MAINE
Cruising the Coast by Car

A Guide Book from
Country Roads Press

MAINE
Cruising the Coast by Car

Arthur B. Layton, Jr.

Illustrated by
Anna Finkel

Country Roads Press
CASTINE • MAINE

Maine: Cruising the Coast by Car
© 1995 by Arthur B. Layton, Jr. All rights reserved.

Published by Country Roads Press
P.O. Box 286, Lower Main Street
Castine, Maine 04421

Cover design by Amy Fischer.
Cover illustration by Cliff Winner.
Illustrations by Anna Finkel.
Text design and typesetting by Pentagöet Design.

ISBN 1-56626-087-6

Library of Congress Cataloging-in-Publication Data

Layton, Arthur B. Jr.
    Maine: cruising the coast by car / Arthur B. Layton, Jr.;
    illustrator, Anna Finkel
    p.   cm.
    Includes index.
    ISBN 1-56626-087-6 : $9.95
    1. Maine—Guidebooks. 2. Atlantic Coast (Me.)—
    Guidebooks. 3. Automobile travel—Maine—Atlantic
    Coast—Guidebooks. I. Title.
    F17.3.L39 1995
    917.4104'43—dc20   94-40886
                                                                CIP

Printed in the United States of America.
10 9 8 7 6 5 4 3 2 1

To Frances Allen

CONTENTS

Introduction

Maine's coastline is as beautiful and fascinating as it is extensive. It stretches from Kittery on the New Hampshire border to Calais beside the Canadian province of New Brunswick. In between, cities and villages that thrived during the heyday of a once flourishing maritime culture are strewn like pearls from a broken necklace, their origins often forgotten.

The intent of this book is to provide an entertaining historical perspective to what you will encounter on the Maine coast, because in many ways coastal Maine is a subculture. That and the coast's pristine scenery provide its charm and make it different from the rest of coastal New England.

In the nineteenth century, Maine's isolated coastal communities were connected to each other and the world by a maritime culture that spanned the North Atlantic from Maine and the Canadian Maritimes to the British Isles and the fjords of Scandinavia. At one point, one-quarter of Maine's male population was in some way involved in shipping and shipbuilding. The economic decline of these world-trading coastal communities began with the emergence of large steamship companies headquartered in major cities.

By the beginning of the twentieth century, the maritime communities across the dome of the North Atlantic were in a wrenching grip of economic decline and, in an effort to survive, turned to tourism. But their maritime culture still lives. In that context coastal Maine shares a stronger commonality with Nova Scotia and the remoter parts of the United Kingdom and Ireland than it does with the more industrially diversified rest of New England.

Traveling Maine's intricately indented, island-studded, 5,200-mile coastline is equivalent to crisscrossing North America. And, just as you pass through different regions driving across the continent, you pass through different regions as you drive along the Maine coast. It is constantly interesting, often fun, and frequently exhilarating. The number of things to do and see can be overwhelming, which is why this book does not list them all nor go into detail about how to get from one point to another. Instead, it attempts to be something of a movable viewing platform as you drive from locale to locale. You can fill in the omissions, which are not major, with a road map and the countless free brochures available at tourist information bureaus. I hope you enjoy the tour. I did.

1
York County

In this region, Maine's storied rockbound coast is not rocky. It is a gradually curving procession of salt marshes and boulder-strewn beaches interspersed by small, craggy headlands that are made prominent only by the low sweep of the shoreline. The biggest gap in Maine's otherwise fortresslike coastline is in York County. This is beach country, as far as Maine topography goes, where most of the people who visit the coast come to play in the sea. Here a series of sun-dappled strands run beside the bend of the Gulf of Maine's Bigelow Bight from Kittery to Portland.

The York County region has the state's highest population density and its biggest summer influx, and it is the only niche in the state's 5,200-mile coastline where natural sand beaches and unnaturally large concentrations of wealth are commonplace. In many respects it is Maine as it is often portrayed in television dramas—a generic composite of what viewers expect—a hauntingly beautiful locale inhabited by people who, with the exception of their accents, are no different from people anywhere else in the United States and where the only people who actually seem to work for a living are commercial fishermen. It is a false image, but if you enter the state on US 1 from the nearly continuous summer playground of the New Hampshire coast, that portrayal of Maine can seem true.

Other than a "Welcome to Maine" sign, your eyes do not light on any striking differences when you cross the old two-lane bridge that carries US 1 over the Piscataqua River from historic

Portsmouth, New Hampshire, to historic Kittery, Maine. But you are entering a state that is culturally and geographically distinct from the rest of New England; the transition takes place gradually as you move east from the Piscataqua River toward the Kennebec River.

The big difference between the opposing banks of the Piscataqua is that there is more to do and see in Portsmouth, an old New England shipping port that has turned itself into an attractive and interesting small city. If you have not seen it, take a spin around town, making sure to visit the restored Colonial section of Strawbery Banke, which in the first half of this century and much of the last one was the city's red-light district. Where mariners and prostitutes once cavorted, restored buildings are now set off by beds of flowers, and the only red lights are the ones that signal motor traffic to halt.

The handsome historic district is conveniently next to the US 1 bridge to Kittery, where the Portsmouth Naval Shipyard is located and where in 1904 the accord that ended the Russo-Japanese War was negotiated. The peacemakers' celebration, however, ran afoul of a Maine prohibition law then in force, and the diplomats were forced to come back across the river to Portsmouth for the champagne with which they toasted their accomplishment. The result was that Portsmouth got the credit for being the site where the treaty was forged when it was only the site where the champagne was poured.

Looking left as you cross into Maine on US 1 above the swirl of the Piscataqua, you can see large commercial vessels lying alongside piers on the Portsmouth side. Beyond, lofted skyward, is the massive steel arc of the I-95 bridge, which most people use to enter the state. Downriver to the right is the low, sprawling outline of the Portsmouth Naval Shipyard, which despite its name is in fact in Kittery, Maine's oldest town. From its inception in 1623, Kittery has been well known for its skilled shipbuilders. In midriver, helping support the US 1 bridge, is Badger's Island, named for William Badger, one of Kittery's earliest and foremost shipbuilders. Small vessels are still built on this island, and as you near the Kittery shore, unless it is winter, you will see a fleet of pleasure craft bobbing at their moorings.

When your wheels touch the mainland in Kittery, you are abreast of Warren's Lobster House, long a popular spot with cruising yachtsmen and motorists. With money to spend, and a right-hand turn onto a side street and another into Warren's parking lot, you can be sitting down to a lobster dinner within ten minutes of entering Maine.

Straight ahead as you come off the bridge from Badger's Island is the John Paul Jones Memorial park with a monument commemorating the launching from Langdon's Island in 1777 of the USS *Ranger.* In this ship John Paul Jones, who had journeyed to the Piscataqua River by coach to take command, carried the news to France of the British defeat at the Battle of Saratoga. As *Ranger,* its colors flying, entered Quiberon Bay on the opposite side of the Atlantic, the French fleet fired in recognition. It was the first salute of the American flag by a foreign nation.

From here, you are in position to get on State 103, which leads by the main gate of the Portsmouth Naval Shipyard. The nation's oldest federal shipyard, it opened in June 1800. Its Command Museum is open to the public by appointment. You pass the yard's original brick and iron main gate as you wind through town toward the modern main gate just outside of Kittery. On the way you pass Rice Public Library, a good example of Victorian brickwork and a fine testament to the now all-but-lost skill of nineteenth-century masons.

Portsmouth Naval Shipyard, which began building wooden warships for the U.S. Navy, now refits, maintains, and repairs the navy's modern submarines. As in the days of wooden shipbuilding, the yard continues to be a major stimulus to the economies on both sides of the river. The steam-powered sloop of war USS *Kearsarge,* which in 1864 sank the Confederate raider CSS *Alabama* in a ferocious sea fight off Cherbourg, France, was launched from this yard during the early years of the Civil War. *Kearsarge* was followed down the ways a few months later by another steam-powered sloop, USS *Ossipee,* which was to play a major role in Adm. David G. Farragut's capture of Mobile, Alabama.

The best part of Kittery is Kittery Point and Gerrish Island, which face Portsmouth Harbor from its north side and are situated next to each other a few miles down State 103 and the Piscataqua River. Kittery Point was once the home of William Pepperell, reputed to have been the nation's first millionaire. His mansion, which was confiscated during the Revolution and later bought back by Pepperell descendants, still stands.

Pepperell's life is a seventeenth-century rags-to-riches story. He came to North America as an apprentice boy in an English fishing schooner, and after his time was up he established himself on the Isles of Shoals, off Kittery Point, where he caught and dried specialty fish for the European market. During his frequent trips to Kittery Point, he met John Bray, an English shipwright who had established a shipyard on the Point, and Bray's daughter, Margery, whom Pepperell married. Pepperell stayed on the mainland and began to put together the largest financial empire in Colonial New England, using fishing and shipbuilding as its foundation. The former apprentice boy called his company The William Pepperells. It built ships on the Piscataqua and Saco Rivers, at whose headwaters were great stands of virgin timber. The Pepperells' story is really the story—on a less grand scale—of the region and the state and why people came here, fishing and shipbuilding. Fish—first for the European market and later for the domestic and West Indian markets—ranged offshore in abundance; lumber for shipbuilding, which could be floated seaward on Maine's many rivers, covered the interior. Kittery was considered ideal for both, particularly shipbuilding. The first British Royal Navy warship built in Colonial America, the 637-ton frigate *Falkland,* was launched from Badger's Island in 1690; it was soon followed by the 372-ton galley *Bedford.* This was the beginning of naval construction on the Piscataqua.

Meanwhile, The William Pepperells had more than a hundred vessels on the fishing grounds and were engaging in a triangular trade with the Southern Colonies, the West Indies, and England, Spain, and Portugal. The company's vessels hauled corn, tobacco, naval stores, fruit, cordage, wines, salt, iron, and dry goods. The company's managers, who were Pepperell's six daughters, invested a portion of the profits in real estate. In the mid–eighteenth century, Pepperell's son, William, led the successful English attack on the French fortress of Louisburg on Cape Breton Island off Nova Scotia. This set the stage for Wolfe's victory over Montcalm at Quebec City, which in turn ended the French and Indian War. Three thousand coastal Mainers from the Piscataqua to the Sheepscot Rivers participated in the taking of Louisburg, from which French privateers had been raiding Yankee shipping. The apprentice boy's son was made a baronet by King George III and became known as Sir William Pepperell.

The easiest public place to find in forested, quietly residential Kittery Point is Fort McClary Memorial Park, which sits on a bluff above Portsmouth Harbor. The site provides expansive views of the harbor, the green and dun-colored lowland of New Castle and its lighthouse tower jutting out from the Portsmouth shore, the wide entrance of the outer harbor, the flash from Whaleback Island Lighthouse, and on the horizon the sand-hued rocks of the Isles of Shoals. Nearby, to the left is Pepperell Cove. The park has the added benefits of a beach and a nearby picnic ground.

The fort, which was ordered built in the late eighteenth century and completed just before the War of 1812, is named for American soldier Maj. Andrew McClary, who was killed at the Battle of Bunker Hill in Boston, shortly after the outbreak of the American Revolution. Additional work was done to the fort in the 1840s when the man from Maine who would be Abraham Lincoln's first vice president, Hannibal Hamlin, served here as a private. Some of the granite blocks that were used to strengthen Fort McClary during the Civil War are still strewn about the grounds.

The reinforcement project was abandoned as outmoded, because of the rapid improvement of weaponry during the Civil War.

But the fort and others protecting the harbor and river were not abandoned, because of the fear of a Confederate attack from the sea. Southern sea raiders ranged from the Gulf of Mexico to Massachusetts' Cape Ann, which is visible from the Isle of Shoals; at least one sea raider ventured well into the Gulf of Maine, capturing a vessel off Mount Desert Rock, halfway to Canada. During World War II, civilian volunteers used the fort to scan the horizon for enemy aircraft and the sea for submarines.

Farther along Route 103 is the actual village of Kittery Point, with the U.S. Post Office on the north side of the road facing Frisbee's Supermarket, Inc., North America's oldest family store, established in 1828. Behind Frisbee's, beside the paved lane to the town pier and just back from it, is Cap'n Simeon's Galley, a year-round restaurant with good seafood at reasonable prices. The dining room and bar overlook aquamarine Pepperell Cove, where pleasure craft and commercial fishing vessels are moored. Farther out is the blue-gray expanse of Portsmouth Harbor, Whaleback Lighthouse, and the broad sweep of the Gulf of Maine. Northerly, if you have a window seat, you can see Fort McClary, on its bluff. Between Cap'n Simeon's and the pier is a small, seasonal lobster cookery with picnic tables beside the water.

To get to Gerrish Island, take a right onto Chauncey Creek Road from State 103. On the way is the Chauncey Creek Lobster Pier. Gerrish Island, accessible by a bridge over Chauncey Creek, is a seaward extension of Kittery Point's quietly genteel atmosphere, only a little more so. Once you cross the bridge over Chauncey Creek, take a right to go to Fort Foster, a town park. The park has just about everything for a pleasing afternoon—beaches, picnic grounds, nature trails, and a baseball field—and it is a spot favored by local wind surfers and scuba divers. Fort Foster, which has commanding views of the harbor and the sea (you can see out to the Isles of Shoals), was built at the northeast entrance to Portsmouth Harbor in 1900 and was added to during World War II.

You must return to the Chauncey Creek bridge from Fort Foster on the same road you arrived. A right turn after you cross the bridge will take you beside Cutts Island and salt marshes, then past the head of Brave Boat Harbor, all of which are worth exploring before you arrive at Seapoint Beach, the other public beach in Kittery Point. Or, you can go straight across the bridge from Gerrish Island, up Gerrish Island Lane, and you will come back to State 103, here called Brave Boat Harbor Road. A right turn will take you to what the Chamber of Commerce calls the Yorks.

York Village, about two miles up the river from York Harbor, is a charming community that became a Royal Colony in 1641 and is the oldest chartered city in the United States. York and inland Berwick were the sites of the first sawmills in New England. In York's historic district is one of the oldest public buildings on the continent, Old Gaol Museum, which was built in 1719 as King's Prison for the then Province of Maine. Also here is Perkins House, where the bulk of the negotiations that resulted in a treaty ending the Russo-Japanese War took place. President Theodore Roosevelt was awarded a Nobel Prize for his role in mediating the peace.

In the early nineteenth century, York Village became a summer destination for the rich, and it still has a comfortable, well-cared-for look. This is the part of the region where palatial summer hotels and genteel bed and breakfasts are visited each summer by returning guests savoring sea and sand. York long ago set itself up to accommodate the summer trade, and it has done a fairly tasteful job of it. Its all but landlocked harbor, formed by the twists of the York River, is a refuge for fishing vessels and yachts every decade or so when major hurricanes sweep along the coast in the fall. York Harbor, at the mouth of the York River, can seem less charming than York Village, but it looks out at the distant wink of Boon Island Light, six miles offshore in the Gulf of Maine. If the wind is right, you can breathe the refreshing pungency of salt air.

During a winter in the eighteenth century, sailors shipwrecked on the bare rock hummock of Boon Island, which is mostly awash at high tide, endured agony and despair as they huddled against the wind in sight of the mainland. Maine novelist Kenneth Roberts wrote a book, *Boon Island,* based on the incident, in which men died from exposure while people ashore, unaware of their plight, went comfortably about their daily routines. Today the rock and its light are used as a mark in offshore sailboat races. Maine is not only a yacht-building locale, it is an increasingly popular cruising ground for yachtsmen, particularly between Kittery and Mount Desert Island to the east, with the biggest concentration of pleasure boats lying between Kittery and Boothbay Harbor.

Houses give way to seaside campgrounds as you drive east from York Harbor on US 1A. Looming ahead is a neatly kept motor-home park with hookups where stainless steel and enameled trailers sit side by side in rows on a knoll overlooking the send of the sea rolling toward boulder-pocked Long Sand Beach below a long seawall that extends to the village of York Beach. Descending the shallow incline of the knoll, US 1A runs beside a long row of beach houses facing the beach from the inland side of the road whose beach side is lined with parking meters. As you enter York Beach, there are large, contemporary-style, resort hotels. Rising above the cluster of eating, drinking, and dancing places that make up the downtown is the landmark, turn-of-the-century Union Bluff Hotel. Turn toward the hotel and you should be able to find your way to Cape Neddick and its lighthouse. Sohier Park, at the end of the cape, and the lighthouse, which is a literal stone's throw away, are surrounded by a suburban-looking development of contemporary summer homes, but the view is marvelous.

Just up the road in the town of Cape Neddick, on the Neddick River, which flows into the sea, is where the transition between the Yorks and Ogunquit begins. You can reach Ogunquit by getting back onto US 1 with its antiques shops and fast-food

On the beach at Ogunquit

shacks, or you can try the back roads to Ogunquit, which wind through wooded residential sections set back from the sea. It has the look of outer suburbia—not what you come to Maine to see, but in summer it's the nicer way to go. Regardless of the season, it provides a more pleasant introduction to Ogunquit than the commercialism of US 1.

Ogunquit is the resumption of beach country. With the exception of crowds in summer, it is as different from York Beach as caviar on croutons is from sardines on crackers. Ogunquit has a large and respected summer playhouse, art galleries, antiques and gift shops, and a raft of restaurants that are patronized by people who dress up when they go out. T-shirts and shorts are not the standard uniform of the day here. However, US 1 goes right through the downtown, which detracts from Ogunquit's sense of style. The town's more attractive sections are toward the water, where trolleys carry people back and forth from the beaches. Not long ago this was a fishing village with some summer residents and visitors. Perkins Cove was regarded as one of Maine's most idyllic spots. It is still worth a visit, particularly for its long-established seafood house, Barnacle Billy's, which now shares the little point of land it sits on with two other restaurants and a paved parking lot. There are still a few fishing boats in Perkins Cove, as well as a well-maintained pedestrian drawbridge, and charter boats that will take you out on the ocean. A popular path, known as Marginal Way, leads from the parking lot and runs behind one of the restaurants and along a cliff face above the sea. It comes out about a mile or so later on the Shore Road, which you took to drive to Perkins Cove. As the path approaches Little Beach, you can see the long strand of Ogunquit Beach and Footbridge Beach facing the sea, with the Ogunquit River flowing behind them. In the far distance is the stretch of Moody Beach (private) in neighboring Wells.

There are seven miles of beaches from Ogunquit to Kennebunkport, many of them elongated islands of sand lying between tidal marshes and the ocean. With the exception of Moody Beach, all are public. On some, side-by-side beach houses face sand, water, and wind, and multicolored kites fly overhead amid the cries of soaring gulls. Beyond Moody Beach, in Wells, trails in the Rachel Carson National Wildlife Refuge, favored by bird-watchers, lead through a white pine forest to a salt marsh.

Kennebunk, on US 1 where it crosses the Mousam River, was a declining lumbering and shipbuilding town in the late 1800s. Around the turn of the century, it transformed itself into a flourishing resort community with an electric trolley system that carried vacationers arriving at the railroad station to casinos and hotels. The community has parks and beaches and a downtown—on the National Register of Historic Places—with an abundance of Federal architecture.

Although Kennebunk has a lot to offer, its flavor is less salty than that of Kennebunkport, on State 9 where it crosses the Kennebunk River. Here the beaches run almost due east toward a cleft in the rocks known as Blowing Cave, which shoots the waves of incoming tides thirty feet into the air. A short distance beyond Blowing Cave is Walker Point, where the coast bends northeastward again.

Kennebunkport is an old resort town of curving streets with weathered, shingled buildings that house antiques, apparel, gift shops, and restaurants. The town has managed to balance resort accommodations with the realities of year-round living. It is worth exploring. The Landing boatbuilding school is located here, as well as a trolley museum and a highly touted summer playhouse. This is where the late Maine novelist Kenneth Roberts lived and wrote, bringing the town national fame with his novels set during the Revolution and the War of 1812. Arundel, Kennebunkport's old name, figured prominently in Roberts's works. The popular 1920s writer Booth Tarkington used to spend summers here living aboard a converted lumber schooner.

A Maine "summer cottage" along Ocean Avenue in Kennebunkport

Longtime summer resident George Bush, former president of the United States, owns the comparatively modest Bush family residence with its discreet security gate at Walker Point on Ocean Avenue. Flanked by rambling summer cottages, partially concealed by landscaping, Ocean Avenue has the look of old money, and the seascapes from it are arresting. It leads to forty-acre Vaughns Island Nature Preserve, which is separated from the mainland by two tidal creeks. For a few hours before and after low tide, you can wade to the island; otherwise you need a boat. Once inhabited, the island now sustains a stand of mixed hardwoods through which you can wend your way on trails to the sea.

Cape Porpoise, the most authentic-looking coastal village in York County, is located just a few miles east of Kennebunkport on State 9. It is generally considered to be the best deepwater harbor between Portsmouth and Portland. Although there are usually yachts in the harbor in summer, Cape Porpoise still has the look of a fishing community. This means few tourist accommodations, but there is a place to eat—Seascapes Restaurant, which has a lovely view of the town's protected harbor.

Farther along State 9 is Goose Rocks Beach, facing Goosefair Bay, and then Fortunes Rocks Beach. Just beyond is State 208, which you can take east to Biddeford Pool, which marks the southern end of Saco Bay.

Nearly an island, Biddeford Pool is connected to the mainland by two tendrils of land. Between them is a mile-wide tidal pool at high tide and, at low tide, a mudflat. The exception is the dredged harbor, whose entrance is the narrow gut through which the tide flows in and out of the pool. The actual tidal pool is known simply as The Pool. The town is a small summer resort and fishing community whose environs are a favorite of bird-watchers. Eclectically designed beach houses give way to traditional coastal houses as you approach the downtown, which consists of a general store, a snack bar, a post office, the Biddeford

Pool Yacht Club, and some old fish shacks, painted white, clustered beside the gut. If you bear right instead of left before the downtown, you should be able to find the thirty-acre East Point Sanctuary, which the Audubon Society maintains for the protection of birds. The shore is rocky here, interspersed by pebble beaches, and trails curve along the edge of the sea and through a meadow. Offshore, to the northeast, is Wood Island and its lighthouse. To the east is the unimpeded blue sweep of the Gulf of Maine, with shafts of sunlight prancing on its surface. Northwesterly is the long contour of Old Orchard Beach; northerly, if your eyes are good, is the distant outline of Prouts Neck, the northern end of Saco Bay.

There is no way out of Biddeford Pool except driving back the way you came. Once back on the mainland, look for secondary roads to the right, which should lead you onto The Pool's northern tendril, where there is a bathing beach—Hills Beach—a few miles below the mouth of the Saco River. There are no bridges across the Saco until you get to the two handsome industrial cities of Biddeford and Saco, opposite each other across the river. On the way to them, you pass the campus of the University of New England, situated above the mouth of the Saco.

Biddeford and Saco (once known as Pepperellborough) were part of The William Pepperells company holdings and were established in the seventeenth century as lumbering towns. After the Revolution and the confiscation of the Pepperells' land by the new government, Biddeford and Saco were expanded; many of the Federal buildings still stand. By the early nineteenth century, the communities' growing economies were stimulated by the establishment of cotton and woolen mills. French Canadians from the Province of Quebec, attracted by steady employment, began migrating here, particularly to Biddeford. The city still has a textile mill, WestPoint Stevens, which produces Martex and Lady Pepperell label towels, sheets, blankets, and bedspreads. You can buy these at the mill's outlet store on Main Street on weekdays. In

Saco, machine guns are manufactured to specifications of the North Atlantic Treaty Organization nations. The downtowns of these cities, with their well-maintained Federal and Victorian buildings, are worth exploring. During the Civil War, Saco and Biddeford were garrisoned to protect them from attacks from the sea by Confederate raiders, which was not a fanciful possibility. In coastal Maine communities, the Civil War caused great economic concern, which proved to be justified, and mixed personal feelings. That may seem odd, because of Maine's remoteness from the South, but there were close ties between the coastal towns and cities of Maine and Southern ports. They had been twisted together by Maine's predominance in the shipping industry and the state's dependence on cotton for its growing number of mills. The personal contacts made by Mainers and Southerners engaged in these enterprises had fostered friendships and marriages.

Unless you are in a hurry to reach Portland, you can delay getting onto US 1 and continue on State 9 down the other side of the Saco River to Camp Ellis and Old Orchard Beach, Maine's impressionistic answer to Coney Island and Miami Beach. Camp Ellis, beside Casco Bay at the mouth of the Saco, is a fishing community without the charm of nineteenth-century architecture. The town, named for the World War I training camp that was once there, looks out at Wood Island Light and the northerly edge of Biddeford Pool.

State 9 swings north of Camp Ellis, and just a few miles after leaving town comes to wooded Ferry Beach State Park, which has nature trails, a picnic area, and a good swimming beach as well as a pond.

Whether or not you like Old Orchard Beach, seeing it is an interesting experience, because it is in almost every way opposite from the popular image of Maine. It's a bit like encountering a rhinoceros in a Saskatchewan snowstorm. State planners and nature preservationists may be aghast at Old Orchard's carnival atmosphere, but its nine-mile, rock-free bathing beach is one of the longest and best strands in New England, and its packed sand surface, varying in width from a quarter to a half mile, is hard enough for automobile racing. On the beach facing Casco Bay is a swath of bungalows interspersed by multistory resort hotels. Roughly in the center is the downtown and its amusement park, all of which is aglitter with plastic signs and neon lights advertising exotic fast foods, electronic games, souvenirs, and computer-generated color portraits. In this town, long a favorite summer resort for French Canadians, French is heard more often on the beach and in the hotels than is English.

Old Orchard Beach is one of Maine's oldest resorts. It got its start in the early nineteenth century when residents of Saco and Biddeford began making day trips there. A residence near the beach was converted to a boardinghouse, and by the 1840s rich families in Montreal were hitching up their carriages for the long ride to Old Orchard and a summer by the sea. The opening day for years was June 26, St. John the Baptist, or Midsummer's, Day, which from pre-Christian times was associated with immersion as a cure for diseases. The observance of Midsummer's Day waned in a changing atmosphere. With the coming of railroads, the sound of hammers on nails resounded along the beach, as resort hotel after resort hotel was constructed for the massive influx of bathers.

After Old Orchard, a series of smaller beaches progresses along the curve of the Saco Bay shore to Pine Point in Scarborough, which is known for its harness racing track. Here, the broad mouth of the Scarborough River flows around Pine Point to the bay, and State 9 swings sharply to the left to rejoin US 1. Along the way, State 9 runs beside 3,000-acre Scarborough Marsh, the state's largest salt marsh, which is popular with nature walkers and canoeists. At Oak Hill on US 1 you can run back down to the coast by taking State 207 to Prouts Neck and Scarborough Beach State Park, which is situated between salt marshes and the sea and has a local reputation for its surf and wide expanse of sand. Because the park is on the outskirts of Portland, on hot summer weekends it is crowded.

By contrast, Prouts Neck, where Winslow Homer once painted, is an uncrowded, exclusive, wooded bluff overlooking the sea. Long a luxuriating spot for rich out-of-staters, it has become, as well, a prestigious, year-round preserve for wealthy Portlanders. One of the most amenable establishments on the coast, The Black Point Inn, is located here. The nearby Prouts Neck Bird Sanctuary, where trails and boardwalks have been laid out in the woods, is surrounded by a private summer colony. It is a lovely place, but parking is not allowed, which means that if you want to tour the sanctuary, you have to leave your vehicle off neck and either walk or bicycle on neck. Or you can stay at The Black Point Inn. Another option is to skip the sanctuary and visit Western Beach, just off the neck, where there is a field, bird-watching, and a sheltered expanse of white sand and dunes. Western Beach is next to Ferry Beach (a different Ferry Beach from the one above Camp Ellis), which has just about everything you need, including a good-sized parking lot. The fine sand beach and bathhouse make it popular with swimmers. There is a pond, a picnic ground, and nature trails through the woods. Either beach is well worth a visit, and the experience may interest you enough to walk or pedal to the bird sanctuary.

Leaving Prouts Neck, you pass by Scarborough Beach State Park again. You can take the interesting way into Portland by turning right onto State 77. It runs by the entrance to Higgins Beach, frequented by day-trippers and bungalow owners from Portland. After looping inland for several miles, State 77 swings seaward to the entrance of Crescent Beach State Park, another popular recreation spot with Portlanders, before curving north toward Portland. Shortly beyond Crescent Beach is the right-hand turn onto Two Lights Road, which leads to the tip of Cape Elizabeth. Here, facing the open sea, are Two Lights Battery, Two

Lights State Park, and Cape Elizabeth Light, one of the most powerful in New England.

The World War II coastal artillery and antiaircraft position, with its observation towers, and the state park were named because of their proximity to Cape Elizabeth Light, which was once known as Two Lights. In 1829, twin light towers were built at the south end of Cape Elizabeth. They were replaced in 1874. Since 1924, only one has been operational, but the name Two Lights adhered to the immediate locale as do barnacles to a rocky shore. The state park, between the battery and the lighthouse, is set back from the steeply sloping rock ledges that confront the sea. The paths and picnic grounds provide sweeping views of the ocean and the vessel traffic coming in and out of Portland.

As you head for downtown Portland, be sure to stop at Portland Head Light, at the north end of Cape Elizabeth and near the entrance to Portland Harbor. Commissioned in 1791 by President George Washington, it was the first lighthouse built in Maine, the state's most famous lighthouse, and one of the nation's most often photographed lighthouses. Its hurricane deck provides a view of Portland and the spectacular panorama of Casco Bay.

2
Portland

Yellowish amber lights reflect softly on the polished wood of bar and walls, and the hazy sunlight of early evening filters through windows into the large, high-ceilinged rooms of Gritty McDuff's, a pub brew house in the heart of Portland's rejuvenated Old Port district. A muffled cacophony of conversations and laughter waft from long wooden tables where men and women drink porter, stout, and McDuff's Best Bitter. Waiters and waitresses bear plates of food to the thumping, low-decibel beat of rock music coming from the bar. Similar scenes of conviviality are transpiring simultaneously at Three Dollar Dewey's and Brian Boru's, two other popular Old Port gathering spots, all within walking distance of each other. On a side street below Gritty McDuff's is Chase-Leavitt, one of the most interesting and serious ship chandleries in the state.

The best way to see the Old Port is to park your vehicle and walk its narrow side streets, which abound with interesting shops and a variety of good to excellent restaurants. The atmosphere is old and salty. You can pick up a walking tour guide of the city at the Greater Portland Landmarks office, 165 State Street, which should not be hard to find, because although Portland may be Maine's most sophisticated and vibrant city, it is not that large. You can also get voluminous amounts of reading material about Portland at the Convention and Visitors Bureau and Information Center, which is located across from Cumberland Wharf on Commercial Street. A marked trail takes you along the waterfront.

Portland's population of just under 65,000 makes it the major city in a state that is made up mostly of small towns and villages. If you are heading Down East, the next city along the coast with the vitality and style of Portland is Halifax, Nova Scotia. The two cities have a cultural affinity and analogous origins. Halifax was built in the early eighteenth century by the British government as a fortress city, "The Gibraltar of the North," from which Crown forces could dislodge the French from North America. Portland, which has accumulated a large number of forts over the centuries, did not have such an instantaneous, nor as ambitious, beginning. It evolved a bit like Topsy.

By the early 1600s the Gulf of Maine was still a bonanza for fishermen from the ports of southwestern England, and their numbers were increasing, to the ire of Amerindians, who began seizing fishing schooners and killing crewmen. Captain Christopher Leavitt, a large landowner in York, conceived the idea of fortifying a well-sheltered harbor for the protection of the English fishing fleet; he recommended what became Portland Harbor. When King Charles I learned of the plan, which included a waterborne police patrol, he ordered all churches in England to raise money for it. Nobody seems certain about what happened to the money that was raised, but it was the beginning of Portland, which grew to be the state's prime shipbuilding location. Although it has since lost much of that traditional Maine enterprise to Bath, Portland remains a major shipping port. Most of its annual tonnage is in the massive amounts of oil brought in by tankers, which pump their cargoes into a pipeline that carries it through hundreds of miles of forests to refineries in Montreal.

Portland remains one of New England's major fishing ports and the state's largest by landings. Although there are a million or more lobster traps in Casco Bay, Portland is also a major shrimp, groundfish, and scallop dragger port. Huge volumes of those species, as well as masses of lobsters, are landed at the Maine State Pier, at the foot of Franklin Street, and the Portland Fish Pier, next to Cumberland Wharf. The Portland Fish Pier, where the Portland Fish Exchange is located, is run something like a cross between a commodity and a stock exchange; prices for Maine fish are set here daily at a public auction.

At 5 Portland Pier is J's Oyster, a harborside oyster bar with a full menu that includes steamed clams. It is one of several good seafood establishments scattered along the waterfront.

Sailboat cruises on Casco Bay are also available from the waterfront. Adjacent to Maine State Pier is Casco Bay Lines, which makes daily, year-round runs to Little Diamond Island, Great Diamond Island, Peaks Island, Long Island, Cliff Island, and Great Chebeague Island in the bay and in summer offers a variety of pleasure cruises, including a nearly six-hour, round-trip cruise to Bailey Island, at the eastern end of Casco Bay. In the same part of the city as Casco Bay Lines is the still-in-use 1872, French Second Empire–style U.S. Customs House.

If you continue east on Commercial Street (it's a good idea to retrieve your vehicle and drive), you will come to the Eastern Promenade and the remains of Fort Allen (1814), from which there are sweeping views of Casco Bay and its islands, many of them fortified during the War of 1812, the Civil War, and World Wars I and II. On the way you will pass the Maine Narrow Gauge Railroad Company and Museum, which is located in a nineteenth-century foundry that once produced locomotives and steamships. The railroad museum was established by The Trust for the Preservation of Maine Industrial History and Technology, which has laid an excursion line track to the Eastern Promenade. Nearby is the site of the former Jones and Laughlin Steel Company wharf and the Bath Iron Works drydock, where large military and commercial vessels are repaired.

At the opposite end of Commercial Street is the International Ferry Terminal, where the Prince of Fundy Cruises Limited's *Scotia Prince* makes regularly scheduled runs to Yarmouth, Nova Scotia. It is a twenty-three-hour round-trip, and once the Panamanian Registry cruise ship is beyond the three-mile limit, its slot-machine gambling casino is crowded with patrons. Above the

*The Old Port along Portland Harbor is a great place
for restaurants, shopping, and antiques*

International Ferry Terminal and west of it is the Western
Promenade, which overlooks the Fore River as it flows toward
Casco Bay. It also overlooks South Portland, where at Spring Point
cargo-carrying Liberty ships were built during World War II.

South Portland is also where the only remnant of an
American clipper ship is preserved. It is the bow section of the
Maine-built *Snow Squall*, which was salvaged in the Falkland
Islands and is housed at Fort Preble. The fort, named for

Commodore Edward Preble, a Portland native and a father of the U.S. Navy, was built in 1808 and restrengthened during the Civil War and Spanish-American War. The fort is now occupied by Southern Maine Vocational Technical Institute, which oversees the preservation of *Snow Squall.* Near Spring Point is a bathing beach and a shore walk. Just over the South Portland border in Cape Elizabeth is Fort Williams and Portland Head Light. Western Promenade on clear days has dramatic views of the White Mountains in New Hampshire.

Most of the piers extending into Portland Harbor date from the mid–nineteenth century, when the old waterfront was filled in to make way for a railroad that connected the eastern and western ends of the city. The physical remains of the city's early maritime history are buried between Fore Street, which ran beside the old harbor, and Commercial Street, along which the railroad tracks were laid. Portland's lost waterfront, not its straightened one, is the one recalled in "My Lost Youth" by Portland native Henry Wadsworth Longfellow (1807–82), whose house on Congress Street is on the city's walking tour.

> *I remember the black wharves and the slips,*
> *And the sea-tides tossing free;*
> *And Spanish sailors with bearded lips,*
> *And the beauty and mystery of the ships,*
> *And the magic of the sea.*

That and "The Shadows of Deering' Woods," now a handsome, wooded public park with paddleboats churning and swans gliding on a pond, were among the poet's remembrances of growing up in Portland. With the glaring exception of the Commercial Street landfill, much of what is in "My Lost Youth" is still recognizable today, particularly Casco Bay and its islands. You can catch some of the lingering spirit of Longfellow's poem in the sweeping views of the bay from the Eastern Promenade.

Unfortunately, Portland's promenades have become a bit seedy, and less safe at night, since Longfellow's day, when life was simpler. People who in the nineteenth century would have lived along the promenades now live outside of Portland along the coast in Prouts Neck, Cape Elizabeth, and, to the east, Falmouth Foreside, Cumberland Foreside, Cumberland, and Yarmouth. The nation's second-oldest yacht club, Portland Yacht Club, is in Falmouth Foreside near Handy Boat, a boatyard that also has a shoreside restaurant, nautical gift shop, and chandlery. The annual end-of-summer, Yarmouth, Maine, to Yarmouth, Nova Scotia, sailboat race originates off the Portland Yacht Club. Down the road beside Yarmouth's Royal River are some good restaurants in and near a marina complex. It might be tricky to find them, but it is worth a try. Beyond Yarmouth is Freeport and Maine's most celebrated store, L.L. Bean.

Suburban Portlanders and city residents go pleasure boating and fishing on Casco Bay, throng to the Portland Museum of Art at 7 Congress Square, and frequent the Civic Center, The Old Port, and Greater Portland's almost nightly concerts. One of the city's biggest attractions is the annual Maine Boatbuilders Show, which is held in the spring and attracts people from all over the Northeast who are interested in finely crafted boats. On warm weekends, city dwellers are running, jogging, and walking on the exercise course that goes around Back Cove. They enjoy Deering Oaks Park, which was designed by Frederick Law Olmsted, who also designed New York's Central Park.

A longtime recreational favorite of residents and visitors is the heavily timbered Portland Observatory at 138 Congress Street, the last remaining nineteenth-century marine signal tower on the East Coast. Built in 1807, the observatory rises 227 feet from Munjoy Hill. From it you can see all the seaward approaches to Portland, and on clear days the White Mountains. It was originally fitted with a powerful telescope so the watchman on duty could identify incoming vessels and, by hoisting signal flags, let the town, particularly the merchants, know. During the War of 1812, the watchman in the tower gave as best he could a blow-by-blow description of the fight near distant Monhegan Island between the American frigate *Enterprise* and the British sloop of war *Boxer*, as a crowd below listened.

Except for a Confederate raid during the Civil War and tension over German U-boat attacks during World War II, this was the last time Portland would be brushed by the harshness of war. Its earlier experiences were brutally direct. Portland was destroyed twice by the French and Indians, and during the Revolution it was bombarded by the British Royal Navy.

By comparison, the Civil War raid was tame, although that was not the intent of Confederate Navy Lt. Charles W. Read, who had orders to burn New England coastal towns and their ships. Read had already taken ten prizes when he slipped into Portland Harbor under a ruse and stole a revenue cutter. It was all he had time to do. After the war, in 1866, Portlanders managed to do what Read had not. They set their downtown afire during a Fourth of July celebration.

West of Portland is Westbrook, an attractive paper mill town, where Rear Adm. Robert E. Peary, the first man to reach the North Pole, once lived. Peary may have been born in Cresson, Pennsylvania, but his parents were from Maine, and they returned with him shortly after his birth. He grew up in and around Portland and later lived on Eagle Island in Casco Bay. He owned five islets in the bay where he kept his polar sled dogs. Despite the place of his birth, Maine claims Peary as its own, because his parents were Mainers. The explanation is contained in the punch line of a Down East joke that is intended as a glimpse into the intricacies of Maine attitudes and thought. The joke, which is not side-splitting, has to do with a family discussion about whether or not a baby born in Maine by New Hampshire parents is in fact a Mainer. The decision is that he is not, and the punch line is, "Just because the kittens were born in the oven does not make them muffins." So much for Pennsylvania's claim to Peary.

3
Freeport, Brunswick, and Bath

This is the region of the Kennebec River, long considered the line of demarcation where the cultural reach of Boston begins to fade and the influence from Down East begins to be felt. At the river's mouth in 1607, *Virginia,* the first vessel built by Englishmen in the New World, was launched from a short-lived colony. It was up the Kennebec nearly 200 years later during the Revolution that the traitor-hero Benedict Arnold led 1,100 men through the wilderness on a daring but unsuccessful attempt to take Quebec City. This is also the beginning of Maine's serrated coastline, the central or midcoast, where fishing villages face the sea at the ends of twisted slivers of land and where the state's two finest public beaches are situated. The midcoast is, to use a Maine phrase, "finest kind." Most everything that is "finest kind" lies below the almost urban stretch of US 1 that runs from Freeport on the west to Woolwich on the east. In between are the distinctive towns of Brunswick and Bath.

Freeport, a shipping community that became a fashionable summer recreation spot, is now Maine's major shopping mecca. It is a town that has been turned into a parking lot–punctuated bazaar of outlet stores clustered about the international mail-order giant L.L. Bean, which is always open. A quiet community twenty years ago, Freeport now has the subsurface frenzy of a casino town where shoppers, rather than gamblers, go from outlet to outlet searching for the jackpot of bargains. Yet, Freeport has managed to retain much of its outward physical charm. With more than a hundred outlets, there is almost literally a store for every taste. A short distance along Main Street (US 1) from L.L. Bean is Jameson Tavern, where in 1820 papers were signed separating Maine from the Commonwealth of Massachusetts and admitting Maine into the Union. Jameson Tavern is still open for business. Farther east along Main Street is a symbol of Freeport's partial success in maintaining its Maine atmosphere: a McDonald's, without golden arches, housed in a Colonial-style building.

Freeport's access to the sea is the Harraseeket River, where at Porter Landing in 1813 the 220-ton, sixteen-gun privateer *Dash* was launched for two Portland merchants. Under a series of masters during the War of 1812, *Dash* sent fifteen prize ships back to her owners before she foundered in a squall on Georges Bank with the loss of her twenty-four-year-old captain and her crew of sixty men. John Greenleaf Whittier, who was a child when *Dash* sank, later wrote a poem about the fast-sailing hermaphrodite-brig titled "The Dead Ship of Harpswell."

Inland from Porter Landing on Upper Mast Landing Road is the Audubon Society's Mast Landing Sanctuary. It is 140 acres of fields, alder-covered lowlands, orchards, and forests where a former millstream spills over its dam and runs through a tidal marsh on its way to the Harraseeket. Trails meander through the sanctuary, which has been set up for picnicking. In Colonial times, tall pine trees were cut at Mast Landing for the warships of the British Royal Navy.

Below Porter Landing along the Harraseeket shoreline is the site of the nineteenth-century Cushing and Briggs shipyard and the residential community of South Freeport. In summer South Freeport, which has a well-protected harbor at the head of Casco Bay, blossoms into a yachting center. The Harraseeket Yacht Club (private) is here, along with several marinas where you can inquire about boat rentals. At least one of them has a chandlery and gift shop.

South Freeport's major landmark is a fake medieval castle tower built of stone whose top is visible above the tree line from the sea and sometimes from roadways as you drive about town. It is all that is left of an otherwise wood-constructed summer hotel that "Maine's Electric Railroad King," Amos F. Gerald, had built in 1903 to promote travel on his Yarmouth to Brunswick trolley-car line, which ran through South Freeport. The wooden part of the hotel burned in 1914, and the trolley-car line disappeared in 1935, swept away by clouds of automobile exhaust and the Great Depression.

Bed and breakfasts abound in this section of the coast, but South Freeport has a particularly nice one, Harborside Bed and Breakfast, which is near the harbor in an 1830 Greek Revival house. Almost beside it is Harraseeket Lunch and Lobster Company, which has views of the harbor and across to Wolf Neck. A short walk from both are Freeport Sailing Adventures, which offers crewed sailing tours of Casco Bay, and Atlantic Seal Cruises, which gives lobster fishing demonstrations as well as nature tours. It throws in a ride around Eagle Island, the summer residence of the late Rear Adm. Robert E. Peary, the first man to reach the North Pole. At the mouth of the Harraseeket on Staples Point, the town of Freeport manages Winslow Park, where you can swim, picnic, and camp.

Admiral Donald B. MacMillan, the educator, Arctic explorer, and sometime associate of Admiral Peary, was born on Cape Cod, but he grew up in Freeport, where he came to live with an older sister after being orphaned. As a young man MacMillan came to Peary's attention when he daringly rescued a group of people whose sailboat had overturned at night in Casco Bay. Peary sought out MacMillan, was impressed by him, and introduced him to Arctic exploration.

The attraction on Wolf Neck is Wolf Neck Woods State Park, through whose woods wafts the refreshing scent of salt air as you walk along groomed trails to the shore. Wooden footbridges lead over gullies and depressions. It's easy walking. You can do it in street shoes, but watch yourself and your shoes along the shore at low tide. Clumps of wet seaweed can be as slippery as grease, and if you do not have a good eye for tidal flats, you can sink up to your ankles in ooze.

Another attraction on Wolf Neck is the University of Maine's experimental farm and sights of Black Angus and Belted Galloway cattle grazing. Some of the Black Angus are part of a University of Maine project. The Belted Galloways chomp the grass of a privately owned farm.

The network of secondary roads between Wolf Neck, Mast Landing, and Brunswick are well maintained and easy to figure out, and make for a much better introduction to Brunswick than does US 1. It is the scenic way to get there, and if you like, you can take a speculative detour down Merepoint Neck between Maquoit and Merepoint Bays to Merepoint.

Brunswick is the home of Bowdoin College, which is the most significant feature of this former mill and lumbering town with the widest main street (Maine Street) in New England. It is also where the Androscoggin River begins its northerly bend into Merrymeeting Bay, a huge freshwater eddy formed by the Androscoggin, the Kennebec, the Cathance, the Muddy, and the Abagadasset Rivers and several streams to create a paradise for boaters, paddlers, naturalists, and duck hunters. Other than during hunting season, it is a haven for thousands of migratory birds. The Kennebec is the only river that emerges intact from this medley of waters; it makes its way to the sea through the neighboring town of Bath.

Settled in 1628 beside the Androscoggin River, Brunswick was named in honor of the British Royal House of Brunswick. At the south end of broad Maine Street is Bowdoin College, named in honor of Massachusetts Gov. James Bowdoin, who was a Harvard graduate. Bowdoin opened its doors to students in 1794 and remains Maine's most prestigious educational institution. Franklin Pierce, fourteenth president of the United States, was graduated in the class of 1824; authors Nathaniel Hawthorne and Henry Wadsworth Longfellow were graduated in the class of 1825.

Harriet Beecher Stowe, who was married to a Bowdoin professor, wrote *Uncle Tom's Cabin* in their house beside the campus. The book that brought Stowe national recognition and heated public fervor against slavery was published in 1852, the same year Joshua L. Chamberlain, who commanded the 20th Maine Regiment in the defense of Little Roundtop at the Battle of Gettysburg, was graduated from Bowdoin. If you saw the movie *Gettysburg*, you know about Chamberlain and the 20th Maine. The Harriet Beecher Stowe House is now an inn and restaurant; the Joshua L. Chamberlain House, opposite the tree-shaded campus, is now a Civil War museum.

Works by painter Winslow Homer, who began his career as an artist-correspondent covering the Civil War for *Harper's Weekly*, hang in the Bowdoin College Museum of Art along with works by twentieth-century painter Andrew Wyeth. National art works are on rotating display in the O'Farrell Gallery; nineteenth-century life is depicted in the Pejepscot Museum in the Skolfield-Whittier House. Also on campus is the unique Peary-MacMillan Arctic Museum, devoted to those two graduates of Bowdoin. In summer the campus reverberates with concerts sponsored by the Maine State Music Theatre and the Bowdoin Summer Music Festival. East of the campus is Bowdoin Pines, a stand of 130-year-old white pines whose branches sough gently in the breeze. Beyond them is the Brunswick Naval Air Station, whose entrance is on State 24 and which was established during World War II to train Canadian pilots and to track down U-boats operating in the North Atlantic. During the cold war, Orion aircraft operating from here in cooperation with Canadian forces in Nova Scotia kept a close watch on Soviet submarine activities.

Before leaving Brunswick it is interesting to know that one of Bowdoin's less-known graduates was the nineteenth-century humorist Seba Smith, who is credited with creating the prototype for the character of Uncle Sam, the long-enduring symbol of the United States. Smith, born in Buckfield, Maine, was graduated with Bowdoin's class of 1818. He started the *Portland Courier*, the first daily newspaper east of Boston, and created a fictional character called Major Jack Downing, through whom Smith lampooned politics with homespun wit. Smith's Major Jack Downing letters became so popular nationally that they generated a spate of cartoons depicting Smith's Down East character, whose visage eventually became that of the Uncle Sam on the "I Want You" recruiting posters of World Wars I and II. Smith's insightful humor set a style that was emulated by the later fictional characters Hosea Biglow, conceived by poet James Russell Lowell, and the character of Mr. Dooley, originated by a Chicago newspaperman. In this century the tradition was continued by the real-life cowboy-comedian Will Rogers.

That data about a past vibrancy, trivia for some, is for filing in your memory banks as you drive down State 123 on Harpswell Neck toward South Harpswell and Potts Harbor. The ride down the neck gets better with each mile, with the best scenery being at the end, somewhat like a dessert of seascapes. On the way, at Harpswell Center, is First Meetinghouse (1757), the state's oldest meetinghouse, which is still in use and which is dedicated to its prominent nineteenth-century minister, Elijah Kellogg, another Bowdoin graduate whose inspirational novels for boys and his "Spartacus to the Gladiators" earned him a national reputation. Opposite the church is an eighteenth-century cemetery where Revolutionary War veterans are buried.

The neck lies between Middle Bay on the west and Harpswell and Merriconeag Sounds on the east, with side roads running off in either direction from State 123. Forests and fields are interspersed with fishermen's houses and modest summer residences, as are the rest of the immediate coastal areas in this region where development schemes have been resisted. Commercial fishermen require low overheads to survive the financial ups and downs made by the whimsies of Mother Nature. The strong stance maintained by the fishermen of Harpswell and Orrs and Bailey Islands against the dubious consequences of gentrifying their communities is largely responsible for the locale's charm. There are, however, not a lot of places to eat, but the restaurants that are here are good. In winter the number of restaurants is trimmed by seasonal closings, but the scenery is often as delicious as it is in summer.

Near the border between West Harpswell and South Harpswell is a side road on the right that goes over to Ash Point, which protrudes into Potts Harbor, and then to Basin Point, which makes up the western end of the harbor. Ash Point is largely summer residential; Basin Point, which with Ash Point forms Basin Cove, has a restaurant, a small marina, and a boat launching ramp. The tidal, whitewater rush of the reversing falls between Basin Cove and Potts Harbor is a favorite of kayakers and canoeists.

Back on State 123 south, Ash Point Cove comes into view. Beside it on the right-hand side of the road is Estes, a large shed of a seafood restaurant. You can look east across Harpswell Sound to the white houses dotting the green slope of Orrs Island. Just inside Estes' barnlike interior is a huge model of what is believed to be the largest schooner ever built, the ill-fated, seven-masted *Thomas W. Lawson,* which in 1907 sank off the Irish coast with only one crew member surviving. The food at Estes, which is open summers only, is not bad and the views are good, if you get a window table. You can also eat outside when there is not a strong wind.

South Harpswell is a spic-and-span cluster of small clapboard houses, all painted white, which nestle on a hillock that faces the sweep of the water in three directions. When wind and sun combine with a low tide, whitecaps gallop across a sea that has been churned aquamarine. There is not much to do here other than savor the beauty, unless it happens to be late August, when the air is filled with the roar of the lobster boat races.

Heading back up State 123, look for the road to the right that takes you across Ewin Narrows at the head of Harpswell Sound to Sebascodegan Island, State 24, and south to Orrs and Bailey Islands, where fishermen still hunt tuna with harpoons. These are "finest kind" villages, with Bailey being the finest of the two. There are water views almost everywhere. Once you are on Orrs Island, you are driving on top of a tree-studded sliver of rock that rises from the sea at sloping angles. You cross over to Bailey Island on the Cobwork Bridge, made of granite crisscrossed on ledges, which allows the tides to flow back and forth between Merriconeag Sound, Wills Gut, and Casco Bay. The bridge is believed to be the only one of its kind in the world. Just over the bridge on the left is Jack Baker's, a small, gray, board-and-batten, year-round restaurant whose dining-room windows overlook Wills Gut and Casco Bay, where fishermen can be seen hauling their lobster traps. If the restaurant can be judged by its steamers, beer, and blueberry buckle, it is "finest kind."

Farther down State 24, a side road runs off to the right and bends around Mackerel Cove, the island's major fishing boat anchorage, where more than a hundred vessels ride at their moorings. The dining room at the Mackerel Cove Restaurant and Marina extends onto a deck that provides superb views of the harbor and Casco Bay beyond. If you are on a tight budget or you just prefer picnicking, there is a small park with picnic tables at the head of Mackerel Cove.

Swinging back up State 24 onto Sebascodegan Island, you can turn right onto the Cundy's Harbor Road down to Cundy's Harbor, another working fishing village, which is situated between Quahog Bay and the New Meadows River—more of a long tentacle of the sea than a river in the traditional sense. Cundy's Harbor looks as if it has begun only recently to emerge into the twentieth century.

There is no way to get over to the Phippsburg peninsula other than going back up to Cook's Corner, then crossing the New Meadows River on either the Bath Road or US 1. Both roads go to Bath, which probably has the largest collection of handsome, stately houses in the state. The city's past and the coast's past are housed in the Maine Maritime Museum complex; the city's present and future are tied up with Bath Iron Works, Maine's last big shipyard and its largest private employer. Bath is the only coastal town that has maintained an unflagging continuity with its past. It began building ships, and its primary industry is still shipbuilding.

Commercial shipbuilding here dates from the mid–eighteenth century. In 1762, the first full-rigged ship, *Earl of Bute,* was launched from the foot of Summer Street. By 1840, Maine had become the wooden shipbuilding capital of the United States, taking over from Boston, which in turn had taken over from New York, because of rising labor costs in that rapidly growing city. But unlike the former capitals of Boston and New York, whose topography and economic complexities had confined shipbuilding to specific waterfront areas, the new shipbuilding capital was spread out along 5,200 miles of coastline from Kittery to Calais. The ring of caulking hammers reverberated in almost every tidal inlet in the state. Bath, because of its three miles of gently sloping Kennebec shoreline, known as the Long Reach, has claimed with some validity that the Long Reach had produced more ships than any other area of comparable size in the world. By the mid–nineteenth century, so many ships had been built and homeported in Bath that there were people in foreign ports who believed that Bath was the name of a nation.

What makes the coast of Maine different from the rest of maritime New England is that Maine was part of a maritime culture that spanned the dome of the North Atlantic. Its remote towns and villages, like those of Maritime Canada, Iceland, the Faeroe and Orkney Islands, sections of Ireland, Scotland, and Wales, and Devon and Cornwall in England, were directly linked to world trade by citizen investment in shipping. Everyone but the town pauper bought shares, often for pennies, in ships being constructed by local shipwrights. When the newly launched vessels sailed under local masters for Europe, Asia, or South America, the entire community anxiously awaited their safe and profitable return. When a savvy captain traded well, the community, from housemaids to the most prominent merchants, made money in proportion to their shares. When a ship was lost at sea, the entire community bore the burden.

The beginning of the end of a yet unparalleled prosperity for Maine communities and those across the North Atlantic dome came with the consolidation of emerging steamship lines in the mid–nineteenth century. Sail-powered community shipping could not compete with the cheaper freight rates being offered by the large, newly formed steamship companies. By the late nineteenth century, financially desperate coastal towns began opening themselves up to summer residents and tourists, as were their remote counterparts all across the North Atlantic. Bath, however, continued to build ships, and when commercial shipping contracts were scarce, the city's shipyards turned to yachts. In 1884, what was then Bath Iron Works Ltd. was incorporated, and one of its early contracts was to build two gunships, *Machias* and *Castine,* for the U.S. Navy. It was the beginning of many Navy contracts that have ranged from torpedo boats to one battleship and finally to modern destroyers and guided-missile frigates. They are built along the Long Reach, where during the Revolution and the War of 1812 American privateers were constructed.

In between Navy contracts, Bath Iron Works has built a variety of first-rate commercial vessels, as well as J. P. Morgan's black and gold yacht *Corsair,* which was launched in 1930 and was later donated to Great Britain by Morgan during World War II. It was Morgan who reputedly quipped about *Corsair's* maintenance bills, "If you have to ask how much it costs, you can't afford it." In 1937, that year's successful America's Cup defender, *Ranger,* was launched by Bath Iron Works.

Now, in summer, *Hardy II,* Maine Maritime Museum's cruise boat, makes fifty-minute narrated tours of the Kennebec River, including a sweep alongside Bath Iron Works. The museum complex, situated below Bath Iron Works between Washington Street and the Kennebec, is the state's premier cultural shrine, and touring it is the quickest way to understand coastal Maine. If you

*A boatbuilder at the Maine Maritime Museum Apprenticeshop
in Bath works on a dory*

want to do it right, spend a day driving around Bath and touring the museum. The Maritime History Building is open year-round, as is the Apprenticeshop (weekdays), where traditional wooden boatbuilding is taught. The museum also includes the Lobstering and the Maine Coast exhibits buildings. The nineteenth-century Percy and Small Shipyard beside the Kennebec is open from late spring to late fall. Picnicking is allowed at designated spots on the museum grounds. In summer and fall you sometimes get a bonus of touring one of the American Sail Training Association's Tall Ships that visit Bath.

State 209 follows the salt marshes south along the Kennebec River down to Phippsburg village. The Parker Head Road runs off to the left and parallels the river's course to the sea, eventually rejoining State 209 as it swings through a broad salt marsh on its way to the mouth of the Kennebec. Here are Popham Beach State Park, the 1607 Popham Colony site, Fort Popham, and Fort Baldwin, all within a few minutes of each other. It is a bonanza of natural beauty and history. The scantiest offering is the Popham Colony site, simply a plaque commemorating the first attempt at English settlement in the Northeast, which failed because of cold-dampened enthusiasm. The colonists had a shipwright among them, and they built and launched the first English vessel in North America, *Virginia of Sagadahock,* in which they sailed back to the home fires of England. The event bore out English explorer Capt. George Waymouth's 1605 observation that Maine had everything at hand to build ships.

Nearby, the crescent-shaped, three-tiered, granite-block structure of Fort Popham, its gun ports facing the mouth of the Kennebec, provides striking views of river, ocean, and, across the fetch of the sea, Seguin Island Light nestling above a rock cliff. The fort was begun in 1861 to protect Maine shipping from Confederate sea raiders, whose psychological impact on New England shipping interests was proportional to the dread inspired by German U-boats during World War II. The reason Fort

Popham has the look of a ruin is that it was never completed. Back from the river and concealed by the woods on Sabino Hill is Fort Baldwin, a World War I–vintage coastal defense installation that is part of Popham Beach State Park. If you climb to the top of the fire control tower, which was added to the fort during World War II, you will be rewarded with truly panoramic views whose foreground includes Popham Beach, a short drive away.

The beach's scrub-pine and dune grass–bordered parking lot is set back from the sea. A slatted wooden walkway undulates over the low dunes to sand and sea as shafts of sunlight sidle across the blue expanse of the Gulf of Maine and flash over the rock outcroppings of Seguin Island.

A few miles west of the beach, down a private road off State 209, is 600-acre Morse Mountain Preserve, where there is a sheltered bathing beach. There are more beaches at Small Point, a popular scenic locale southwest of Popham Beach that you get to by turning off State 209 onto State 216 and following it to its end. Farther up the west side of the peninsula is West Point, which is roughly opposite Bailey Island, and the fishing villages of Sebasco Estates and Sebasco, which are roughly opposite Orrs Island. The only way off the peninsula is to backtrack up State 209 to Bath.

Across the Kennebec from Bath, in Woolwich, State 127 heads south off US 1 and meanders across Arrowsic Island and Georgetown Island to Reid State Park, where the wide mouth of the Sheepscot River meets the Gulf of Maine. On the way down or back, you can explore Squirrel Point Light, which from the Arrowsic Island shore faces Phippsburg across the Kennebec. It's the white light tower you could see from State 209. The nineteenth-century light is often seen in photographs of newly fitted-out Bath Iron Works' fast frigates as they head downriver for sea trials in the Gulf of Maine. The Old Stone School House Museum is another place on Arrowsic Island to visit. Both Arrowsic and Georgetown abound in salt marshes and bogs. On an elongated piece of granite beside State 127, a wildlife-inspired graffiti artist has painted a bobcat-sized green turtle.

On Georgetown Island are popular spots Bay Point, roughly opposite Fort Popham, and Five Islands, on the Sheepscot opposite Southport Island and the Boothbays. Another is Robinhood, named for a Colonial-era Indian chief, where there is a marina and a restaurant overlooking the Sasanoa River, Westport Island, and Goose Rock Passage. It is a tranquil setting for dinner and the food is excellent, which makes it a nice place to stop after exploring the island.

Near the turnoff to Reid State Park is the 400-acre Josephine Newman Sanctuary, whose trails lead beside cattail ponds, through woods, over ledges, and beside inlets of the sea. The turn from State 127 into the secondary road that leads to Reid State Park is marked by a Department of Transportation sign and, if you are headed east on State 127, by a large rock painting of a red, white, and blue American flag. Reid is one of the most beautiful state parks on the coast, with a superb beach, dunes, a warm saltwater pool, marshes, ledges, and wending trails. There is even a snack bar that specializes in seafood at Todd Point, where sportfishermen cast their lines from the rocks. Two mottled dun and brown sand beaches stretch about a mile and a half between Todd Point and the rocky knoll of Griffith Head, whose landward slope is arrayed with beach roses and wind-stunted spruce.

Heading back to US 1 in Woolwich has the compensation of continuing on State 127 north to Day's Ferry, then turning left onto State 128 for another look at Merrymeeting Bay and the Robert P. T. Coffin Wildflower Reservation. Its trails pass through a mixed forest that overlooks the bay.

Back on US 1, the township of Woolwich lies between the Kennebec and Back River, which eddies back and forth between the town of Wiscasset and the Sheepscot River to the north and a conjunction of smaller tidal rivers to the south. The Montsweag area can be interesting to drive around, if time and fuel are not important considerations. So is Westport Island, a long piece of coastal jigsaw that is formed by Back River, the Sheepscot River, the Sasanoa River, and Goose Rock Passage. (Take State 144 off US 1 and over the high bridge across Back River.) There is not much on the island except trees and water views, which for some people is just fine.

4
Wiscasset, Boothbay, and Pemaquid Point

Wiscasset, a former deepwater port situated along the west bank of the Sheepscot River near the head of tide, is Lincoln County's shiretown. Because of the architecture of its shops, restaurants, and inns, it is arguably the handsomest town bisected by US 1, which is also its main street. Wiscasset is an artists' colony, an antique buffs' paradise, a summer recreation spot, and a bedroom community for commuting Bath Iron Works employees, as well as the site of Maine's only nuclear power plant, Maine Yankee. The payroll of the discreetly located power plant and its huge annual tax payment to Wiscasset are two reasons why the town probably looks more prosperous than it did during its heyday of lumbering and shipbuilding.

Beside the town's waterfront, the remains of the hulks of *Luther Little* and *Hesper* are symbolic of the change in Wiscasset, as is the town's once bustling customhouse, at the end of Water Street. The *Luther Little* and *Hesper* were able sailing vessels that during World War I carried lumber, before their careers ended in 1932 during the financial havoc of the Great Depression. They are moored where they were left, slowly crumbling testaments to Wiscasset's maritime past and the subjects of countless photographs.

As is the rest of the central coast, Wiscasset is bed-and-breakfast country with a smattering of historic tours and tourist attractions. On Federal Street is the Old Lincoln County Jail (1811) and Museum. On Warren Street is the Maine Art Gallery, which displays the works of Maine artists. On High Street are the haunted 1807 Castle Tucker House, the 1811 Wood-Foote House, the 1804 Carleton House, and an 1852 sea captain's mansion that is now the Musical Wonder House. It contains the results of one man's lifetime hobby, the restoration of music boxes. They all work and most of them are antiques. At the town landing near Water Street, the Maine Coast Railroad excursion line takes passengers along the salt marshes of the Sheepscot River. It is particularly popular during the fall foliage season.

Across the river at Davis Island in Edgecomb is Fort Edgecomb, completed in 1809 when war hawks in Congress were pressing for a fight with Great Britain. The original, octagonal blockhouse and earthworks that remain are now part of a state park. Edgecomb is a rural, residential town that sprawls between the Sheepscot and the Damariscotta Rivers above Boothbay. There are mussel and oyster farms along the Damariscotta River. Down the Sheepscot from Fort Edgecomb is the showroom of A. G. A. Correa, a maker of finely worked, nautically inspired jewelry that is as expensive as it is beautiful. Like the A. G. A. Correa showroom, the best parts of Edgecomb are along the side roads that lead off US 1 and State 27, which runs from US 1 to Boothbay Harbor.

Speedy lobster boats and ponderous fish draggers go full bore down the race course in Boothbay Harbor, sending slow, rolling, viscous wakes to slap against the pilings and floats along the shore. Sunlight flashes on rigging and water and then retreats as gray-dappled clouds sweep overhead, releasing wind-driven bursts of wet snow and face-stinging cold rain. Spectators of the first lobster boat race of the season turn up their coat collars and return their hands to their pockets. It is spring in Boothbay Harbor and this is a largely local crowd having a fling before the shorts and T-shirt–clad summer crowd arrives, as it has been in varying garb for nearly a century.

Boothbay Harbor and its region handle the seasonal flow of tourists with the aplomb of sea gods and goddesses directing the tides that daily rush in and out of the hundreds of small estuaries and inlets of this Lincoln County section of the central coast. The Boothbays, at the end of a peninsula, face the sea in a configuration resembling a lobster with extended claws, formed by Southport Island and Linekin Neck. The head, Boothbay Harbor, is an old fishing community whose working waterfront has largely given way to the inns and restaurants of a fashionable summer resort.

Boothbay Harbor teems with charter boats, which range from sailing vessels that cruise the outer harbor to deep-sea sportfishing craft. In summer, excursion boats churn in and out of the harbor laden with passengers on puffin, seabird, and whale-watching trips, as well as lobster fishing demonstrations. In summer, a boat leaves regularly for Monhegan Island, a historic seamark, eleven miles offshore. In July during the annual Boothbay Harbor Days celebration, Maine's classically lined, gaff-rigged, passenger-schooner fleet tacks back and forth in a day race that is followed by passenger-jammed excursion boats. Throngs of people crowd the Boothbay Harbor shore and cluster at points along Southport Island and Linekin Neck to watch the harbor come alive with the large, crisply painted wooden sailing vessels heading for the finish line inside the harbor, as seagulls wheel and shriek overhead. The end of July, usually during the last week of the month, is when the annual, three-day Friendship Sloop Races are run off Boothbay. Again passengers line the rails of excursion and spectator boats along the race course to watch the original gaff-rigged, turn-of-the-century lobster boats and their replicas compete for Friendship Sloop Society awards. In August is the Annual Tuna Tournament.

Because of its tourist industry, Boothbay has sprawled inland (the Boothbay Railway Village on State 27 offers steam train rides through a recreated New England village), but the old town hugs the water and for the most part it is an easy walk. During the peak season of August, it is a good idea to park your car before you get to downtown Boothbay Harbor and, with a map from the Chamber of Commerce Information Center (it's on the way into town), walk the streets. There is a jumble of seafood restaurants, ethnic cuisine restaurants, harbor-view bars and cocktail lounges, shops, and charter boat offices along Commercial Street, House Hill, Wharf Street, By-Way, and Townsend Avenue. The footbridge over the upper harbor leads to Atlantic Avenue where there is a motel, a hot dog stand, a fishermen's cooperative, and vantage points to watch the lobster boat and sailing races.

During the Revolution, Paul Revere stopped here in company with Commodore Dudley Saltonstall of the Penobscot Expedition, which had been dispatched from Massachusetts to dislodge the British garrison at Castine in Penobscot Bay. Saltonstall and his fleet of forty vessels, many of which were privateers that had been unwillingly pressed into service along with their crews, arrived in Boothbay Harbor to take aboard promised reinforcements of local militia. The reinforcements were not as numerous as promised (the Revolution was not popular east of Portland), but Saltonstall took what he could get and set sail, allowing a large number of able-bodied men to come out of hiding. It was not a great moment for the Revolution, but it was a big event for Boothbay Harbor, which was then known as Townsend.

Boothbay has two marine research facilities located beside each other at McKown Point, off State 27 in West Boothbay. Bigelow Laboratory is a privately operated firm whose activities include scientific research in the Gulf of Maine for government agencies and private industry. Next door to Bigelow and overlooking Boothbay Harbor is the Maine Department of Marine Resources Aquarium and a research center that studies the Gulf of Maine and its fisheries. The Department of Marine Resources regulates commercial fishing within Maine's three-mile, jurisdictional limit. (The U.S. Department of Commerce regulates commercial fishing beyond the three-mile-limit line.) The state aquarium and research center's library are open to the public. Whether

Boothbay Harbor, where fishermen and pleasure boaters both find moorings

or not you are interested in science, McKown Point offers a splendid view of Boothbay Harbor, and it is a good place for a picnic.

State 27 continues south over a swing bridge to Southport Island, a site that was being used by English fishermen before the Pilgrims established themselves at Plymouth. The island's east side faces Burnt Island Light. On the island's west side is Hendricks

45

Head Light, washed by the Sheepscot River and Sheepscot Bay. Southport Island is a pacific blend of summer residences and fishermen's houses sheltered under a canopy of trees. State 27 runs across the north end of the island and down its west side through West Southport to Newagen, at the island's southern tip. The light that can be seen offshore is The Cuckolds, named for the two tiny islands it marks. Here in Newagen, State 27 merges with State 238, which runs up the east side of the island, with plenty of side roads to explore.

Piracy is a subject that is ignored generally in histories of Maine, probably because one person's pirate is another person's privateer. Commercial fishermen were Maine's pioneers and in the lawlessness of life on the frontier pirates followed to prey on them, a bit like cattlemen and rustlers in the Old West. Cod may not have been Spanish gold, but it was valuable cargo, and it was not uncommon for pirates to board fishing vessels bound for ports in old England and New England. As the struggle between England and France for control of North America heated, privateers from New France and New England began taking each others' shipping, and the raiding continued after the formal wars ended. During the Revolution there was a resurgence of privateering as Revolutionaries and Loyalists put to sea in a sporadic civil war afloat. Afterward, during the 1790s French pirates returned as the United States and France fought an undeclared war at sea. Vessels from Boothbay and other Maine ports were involved in what, until the close of the War of 1812, amounted to 200 years of intermittent warfare at sea. It was during the War of 1812 that one of its dramatic incidents off the Maine coast was witnessed from Boothbay Harbor and Ocean Point at the tip of Linekin Neck, Boothbay's easterly claw. It was the fight between the U.S. warship *Enterprise* and the British warship *Boxer* off Monhegan Island in which both captains were killed. The residents of the Pemaquid Peninsula turned out to watch as well.

In New England the War of 1812 was an odd war in that the federal government in Washington and its trade embargo, particularly for shipping interests, often seemed to be more the enemy than the declared one, Great Britain. Because of the feeling in New England, British warships were lax about enforcing their blockade of the United States' East Coast, and some British skippers, for a price, would run escort for Yankee vessels returning to port with contraband. That is what *Boxer* was doing when she ran afoul of *Enterprise* by firing her guns off the mouth of the Kennebec River to make the garrison at Fort Popham believe that the smuggling schooner heading upriver to Bath was being chased back into port. Fishermen off Portland heard the cannon fire and reported it to *Enterprise*, which, unbeknownst to *Boxer*, was prowling for it. After the fight off Monhegan, both captains were buried in adjacent graves in Portland's old Eastern Cemetery.

The way to Linekin Neck and Ocean Point, the easterly claw of the Boothbays, is State 96, which passes through East Boothbay, where in 1921 the Arctic exploration schooner *Bowdoin* was launched from Hodgdon Brothers Shipyard for Adm. Donald B. MacMillan. Maritime skills still flourish inside the cavernous boatbuilding sheds of Washburn & Doughty and Goudy & Stevens. Washburn & Doughty builds large offshore fishing vessels and ferries for the Maine State Ferry Service. Goudy & Stevens restores and builds large yachts. Just up the beach rose–bordered street from the shipyards is the studio of a marine artist. Almost on top of the yards in East Boothbay's tiny downtown are Lobstermen's Wharf and Sailmaker's Inn. East Boothbay has a quiet charm that continues over the swing bridge that takes State 96 onto Linekin Neck, where there is another seaside inn at Ocean Point and a view of Ram Island Light, offshore. Linekin Neck is bounded on the west by Linekin Bay and on the east by the Damariscotta River. Pemaquid Point, to the east, is visible from Ocean Point. South Bristol can be seen across the Damariscotta from East Boothbay. The way to them is back up State 27 to the River Road, which leads into Newcastle and Damariscotta. It is a way to avoid returning to US 1.

Newcastle has an inn and a large antiques shop. It is also the home of Bruce King Yacht Design, which recently drew the lines for a seventy-foot production sloop for The Hinckley Company in Southwest Harbor, farther Down East, and for a seventy-nine-foot yacht that cuts through the water at thirty-five knots and was built by Hodgdon Brothers in East Boothbay. Much of what used to be done at a drafting table is now done on a computer with marine design software supplied by Aerohydro, Inc., in Southwest Harbor.

Newcastle faces downtown Damariscotta across the span of the Damariscotta River. Because of the narrowness of the river here and the continuity of the architecture, the towns blend. Damariscotta has a look of fashion and finance to it, particularly in its residential sections. It is also the headquarters of the Maine Aquaculture Association. The Damariscotta River is where much of Maine's multimillion-dollar oyster and mussel industry is concentrated. Oyster and mussel farms are situated in Edgecomb, Newcastle, Damariscotta, and South Bristol. They compete in the U.S. market and abroad with mussels from Spain, China, The Netherlands, Italy, Denmark, and France, and with oysters from Korea, Japan, France, and the West Coast of the United States. Experiments with aquaculture were begun in Maine before World War II when Belon oysters from France were successfully transplanted in the state's estuaries, but most of the mussel, oyster, salmon, and sea trout operations that are spread the length of the coast did not get under way until the 1960s and 1970s. Interest in them was generated partly by Norwegian and Canadian aquaculture firms intent on expanding their share of the U.S. market. Maine, with its many clean, cold estuaries and its nearness to major markets along the Boston-Washington corridor, is considered a natural for aquaculture enterprises.

There are Damariscotta Region Information Bureaus in Newcastle on US 1 and on the business route (US 1B) at the eastern edge of downtown Damariscotta, whose Main Street (US 1B) is dominated by two-story, red-brick commercial buildings hung with brightly painted signs.

Above Damariscotta, at Damariscotta Mills, is The Rockport Apprenticeshop, which used to be in Rockport and which builds classic wooden boats. Its long, sleek, eighteenth-century rowing boats, known as Bantry Bay boats or French officer's gigs, have been demonstrated to the delight of crowds at international maritime celebrations at the Statue of Liberty in New York and off the coast of France. The Apprenticeshop's larger vessels are hauled overland to Damariscotta, where they are launched into the Damariscotta River from the municipal parking lot.

Below Damariscotta is more of the beauty that draws people to the coast, particularly at Pemaquid Point, South Bristol, and Christmas Cove. State 130/State 129 leads south from Damariscotta; then the road splits, with State 129 running southwesterly through Walpole, where the University of Maine's marine research station, The Darling Center, is situated. Walpole is also the location of the oldest church in Maine that still has religious services, the 1772 Walpole Meeting House. State 129 continues down to South Bristol and Christmas Cove, which face Pemaquid Neck and Pemaquid Point across Johns Bay.

State 130 runs over to Bristol and down the middle of the peninsula to New Harbor and Pemaquid Point, which is one of the most strikingly dramatic spots on the coast.

South Bristol is a pleasing fishing village with well-kept houses, a view across the Damariscotta River to those large boatbuilding sheds at East Boothbay, and a swing bridge that takes State 129 over to Rutherford Island and Christmas Cove, so named, the story goes, because Capt. John Smith lay at anchor here on Christmas Day 1614, but no one seems to know for certain. A yachting haven, Christmas Cove is situated on a slender finger of land that protrudes toward Inner Heron Island, Thread of Life Islands, and Thrumcap Island. The coast of Maine has hundreds of thrumcap islands, named by seventeenth- and eighteenth-century mariners because they were small, or about the size of a thrumcap—the equivalent of a modern-day watchcap. The drinking and dining deck of the Coveside, an inn and restaurant at Christmas Cove, is not much larger than a thrumcap, but it is a very pleasant spot to have something to eat and drink and watch cruising boats and daysailers maneuver in and out of the harbor. If you are interested in buying or renting a boat, a yacht brokerage office is in the same building as the restaurant.

To get over to Pemaquid, double back on State 129 to West Bristol, then turn right onto the Pemaquid Road, which runs into the Old Harrington Road and State 130. There is not a lot in Harrington other than the eighteenth-century Harrington Meeting House, in which eighteenth-century graffiti, uncomplimentary to the minister of the period, was discovered when the meetinghouse was being restored in the 1960s.

The part of New Harbor that lies astride State 130 is a commercial district that caters to the summer trade, where you can browse and get take-out sandwiches. On the west side of the district is Pemaquid Beach State Park, where for a small admission fee you can loll in real sand and swim in Johns Bay, which is shallow and therefore relatively warm. Almost around a corner from the beach is Colonial Pemaquid and the remains of Fort William Henry (later named Fort Frederick), a historic site maintained by the state's Bureau of Parks and Recreation.

English settlers began arriving at this fishing and fur-trading station in the mid-1620s, establishing one of the most northerly settlements in New England. As more English moved in, the Abenaki Nation became alarmed about the strangers in their midst. So did the French, who encouraged the fears of the Abenakis and poured gunpowder on the smoldering embers of war. The Abenakis burned the village at Pemaquid in 1676 and again in 1689, after it had been rebuilt and fortified with Fort Charles, the first of three forts built here. The second was Fort William Henry, New England's first stone fortification, complete with towers. The French and the Abenakis leveled it in 1696.

That was the end of Pemaquid until 1720, when a group of Protestant Irish from southern New England resettled the site and erected Fort Frederick over the ruin of Fort William Henry. The tower there today is a replica, but the archeological digs beside the fort and at the nearby site of old Pemaquid are genuine, and the state museum at the site village is engrossing. Next to the museum is a reasonably priced restaurant.

Pemaquid Point and Pemaquid Point Lighthouse and its Fishermen's Museum are at the end of State 130. The point, part of a state park (small admission fee), is a visual pot of gold at the end of a scenic rainbow. The point runs out into the sea like an exposed rib of the earth. From it and the lighthouse grounds you have an unimpeded view of the Gulf of Maine. Monhegan is the large island to the southeast; due east are the Cushing and St. George peninsulas and the Georges Islands. To the west are Christmas Cove, South Bristol, and Linekin Neck.

The most scenic main route on the peninsula is State 32, which heads east off State 130 a few miles north of Pemaquid. It runs through the most appealing section of New Harbor, a snug fishing village that embraces a working harbor. Here you can eat moderately priced lobsters at picnic tables beside the fishermen's cooperative or more expensive lobsters, accompanied by beer or wine, at Shaw's while you wait for the next boat run to Monhegan Island.

On State 32 north toward the summer village of Chamberlain is the small Rachel Carson Salt Pond Preserve. Chamberlain is an interesting little community clustered around Long Cove (marvelous views). The only noticeable nonresidential structures are a post office, a tennis court, and a bed and breakfast. Several miles up the road is Round Pond, whose village, facing Muscongus Sound, is one of the most charming on the coast. It once was abustle with granite quarrying and the activity of several fish processing plants. With the exception of a boatyard, a seafood restaurant beside the harbor, and a fishermen's cooperative, it is now a summer retreat for artists and writers. From here, Capt.

Harry B. Harden offers sight-seeing seaplane flights along the coast at reasonable prices. Look him up; he is in the telephone book. Flying along the coast puts all those bays, coves, and inlets in perspective. It's almost better than sailing. At Muscongus you can take the Old Shore Road, which runs along Greenland Cove to Medomak, where at the foot of Keene Neck there are two Audubon Society–supported areas— Hockomock Nature Trail (self-guided shore walk) and Todd Wildlife Sanctuary, a nature study area located on Hog Island below Keene Neck. About a twenty-minute drive north of Round Pond is the town of Bremen, which faces a maze of islands and inlets where the Medomak River meets the incoming tide from Muscongus Bay and which contains several villages that are little more than crossroads.

Farther up State 32 is Waldoboro, named for Samuel Waldo, an eighteenth-century land speculator, a brigadier general in the colonial militia, and a hero of the French and Indian War. He helped dislodge the French from their fortress at Louisburg, Nova Scotia, which set the stage for the English conquest of North America. In the 1740s he induced a group of Germans from the Palatine Electorate on the Rhine to settle on land that he had acquired in Maine. Waldo's extensive acreage came to be known as the Waldo Patent, and in it Waldo established a colony for the Protestant Germans at Broad Cove, which is bordered by Bremen and Waldoboro. About a mile south of Waldoboro beside State 32 is the Old German Church (1772) and the German Protestant Cemetery.

Waldo County, to the east, which was once much larger, is also named for the hero of Louisburg. The Germans he brought to Maine came to be known as Waldo Germans, and many of their descendants formed militia units in support of the American Revolution.

Waldoboro is a former granite-quarrying and shipbuilding community with an attractive brick and granite commercial district and the interesting Waldoboro Historical Society Museum. Perhaps the town's most popular distinction, other than having helped supply granite for the construction of Radio City Music Hall in New York City, is as the home of Moody's Diner, at the top of a hill near the junction of US 1 and State 220. Moody's became something of a landmark, a coastal halfway house, for World War II–era motorists traveling US 1 for business and pleasure. The food was native, good. It still is.

5
Thomaston to Rockland and Offshore

In 1605, Capt. George Waymouth sailed into the St. George River, shanghaied five Indians, and began teaching them English on the voyage back to England. From these halting conversations, Waymouth later released such glowing reports about the wooded, gently rolling peninsulas of Cushing and St. George, below present-day Thomaston and Rockland, that by the 1630s Englishmen were settling in the region. Years earlier, Waymouth had returned the Indians who had survived the new diseases and vices of England to Maine. One of them, Samoset, who remained a traveler, greeted the Pilgrims arriving in Plymouth in 1620 with the words, "Much welcome, Englishmen."

People continue to come and go here, drawn by word of mouth, the canvases of nationally acclaimed artists, and the seagoing ferries that ply between mainland ports and the islands of Monhegan, Matinicus, Vinalhaven, and North Haven.

Thomaston, at the head of the tidal portion of the St. George River, was incorporated in 1777. By the nineteenth century its Shore Village section, facing nearby Penobscot Bay, had become so prosperous from shipbuilding and lime trading that it broke away and was renamed Rockland. By midcentury, Rockland was the shiretown of the new county of Knox, which was named in honor of Maj. Gen. Henry Knox, a Thomaston resident, entrepreneur, and Revolutionary War hero whose exploits are included in the celebration of Patriot's Day, a Maine and Massachusetts holiday. Knox's bent for business speculation set an enduring style for the region.

Montpelier, a replica of the general's Georgian-style mansion, sits on a knoll beside US 1 on the east side of Thomaston. The huge white clapboard house is not inappropriately almost cheek by jowl with the Dragon Cement plant's two huge, dusty lime quarries that straddle US 1.

Knox, among other things, was the region's best-known manufacturer of lime, which then and now is used to make mortar and cement. The general was convivial, enjoyed the play of light on robust colors, juggled multiple business enterprises until his death in 1806, and lived beside a mile-wide vein of limestone that runs from Thomaston through Rockland and Rockport, and peters out someplace between Camden and Lincolnville. It is Maine's only significant limestone deposit. Lime, granite, shipbuilding, shipping, and fishing have been the bulwarks of the region's economy and a source of romance to enhance its tourist industry. Except for tourism, Knox dabbled in them all.

He was born in Boston in 1750, married a daughter of Loyalists who later inherited much of the land in Knox County, and became Gen. George Washington's artillery officer. It was Knox who, as a colonel in the Continental Army, sledded cannon over 300 miles of snow from Fort Ticonderoga in upstate New York to Dorchester Heights in Boston, tipping the scales in favor of the besieging Americans and forcing the British to evacuate Boston on April 17, Patriot's Day. After the Revolution, Knox became the new nation's first secretary of war. In 1795, he retired to Thomaston and began building Montpelier while launching numerous financial ventures that at one point included an eighteenth-century version of an industrial park on Sears Island in Upper Penobscot Bay. Knox died before any of his enterprises turned a profit, and Montpelier fell slowly into disrepair and eventually was torn down in 1871 to make way for a railway. The Daughters of the American Revolution and the Knox Memorial Association had the replica built in 1930. It is being restored with the help of prisoners from Maine State Prison, which is on the west side of town over the eighteenth-century site of Maine's first lime manufacturing operation. (The prison more or less marks the beginning of the region's limestone vein.) Montpelier, filled with period antiques, and with rooms whose wallpaper has been reproduced from remnants of the originals, is open from Memorial Day to Labor Day, Wednesdays through Sundays.

Thomaston's main street (US 1) is lined with tree-shaded, historic houses. Inside a granite-trimmed brick commercial building, a short distance from the prison in the direction of Thomaston's nineteenth-century brick and clapboard commercial district, is the Maine State Prison Showroom Outlet, which sells ship models and a variety of furniture and gifts. The store's side street windows face a white clapboard sandwich and ice cream shop, which has an array of flowers blooming by its entrance.

From the south side of this section of Main Street, side streets flanked by Federal, Greek Revival, and Victorian houses, many of them shipwright-built, lead downhill to Water Street, which curves along a still-active, once-vibrant waterfront where yachts rather than commercial sailing vessels are now built. Boatyards, the town landing, and a waterfront restaurant are scattered along Water Street from Lyman Marine Services and the former Wallace Shipyard at the foot of Knox Street to Jeff's Marine on the east side of the St. George River.

Thomaston is quiet, but it was not always so. In 1780, during the Revolution, a Loyalist from Damariscotta who was convicted of guiding a British foraging party from Castine through the region was hanged from gallows on Limestone Hill. Another convicted Loyalist, Gen. Peleg Wadsworth, who was being held prisoner in the barn of the Revolutionary militia commander for the area, escaped. Shortly afterward the British garrison at Castine dispatched a raiding party to Thomaston and, after a firefight at the general's home on Wadsworth Street, captured him and took him to Castine. Several months later, General Wadsworth, the grandfather of poet Henry Wadsworth Longfellow, escaped, again.

Near Jeff's Marine, the River Road winds down the Cushing peninsula to Cushing and the Olson House, where Andrew Wyeth painted the much-acclaimed *Christina's World*. In Cushing a series of back roads runs down to Hawthorne Point, Maple Juice Cove, and Pleasant Point, where across the mouth of the St. George River there are angled views of Port Clyde and a small maze of islands marching seaward toward Monhegan Island. It was at Maple Juice Cove in the 1780s that Loyalist Waldo Dicke commandeered a Boston-bound vessel laden with lime and sailed it to Castine.

Olson House is well worth a look, particularly if you have a romantic streak, but most of the fields that were there when Wyeth painted are now covered by trees. The ride to Olson House can be more pleasing than arriving there. The peninsula is dotted with hill crests rising above hayfields that undulate softly toward patches of forest and blue vistas of the St. George River. Cushing is less visited than the St. George peninsula, and there is no place to buy food, which could be unfortunate, if you are hungry.

At the lower end of the Cushing peninsula, on State 97, is Friendship, a lobster-fishing community celebrated for having produced the Friendship sloop. This turn-of-the-century, gaff-rigged lobster-fishing boat has graceful lines and looks like a bird on the wing when all the boat's sails are flying in a fair wind. Muscongus Bay is the town of Friendship's biggest asset. Drive around to seek out appealing viewing spots.

Friendship sloops evolved from Muscongus Bay sloops, earlier nineteenth-century lobster-fishing boats. Friendship sloops and variants of them were used up and down the coast and were constructed by a variety of builders, but they came to be called Friendship sloops because a man who built a lot of them, Wilbur Morse, had his shop in Friendship. The Friendship Sloop Society, made up of sloop owners from all over the Northeast, has a sail-by here in late July, which coincides with the society's Friendship Sloop Races off Boothbay Harbor.

State 97, which joins US 1 at South Warren, is the fastest way back to Thomaston from Friendship.

From the east side of Thomaston, the turnoff for Montpelier (State 131) runs down the St. George peninsula to Port Clyde, passing through St. George village, Tenants Harbor, and Martinsville. Port Clyde is a respectable fishing village that over the years became rouged up for tourists waiting to board the privately owned, sixty-five-foot, former Army tugboat *Laura B,* which makes daily trips to Monhegan Island. Before boats began running from New Harbor and Boothbay, the Port Clyde boat was the only one running to the island. Now with summer congestion for its Monhegan boat reduced, there is less pressure on the natural charm of Port Clyde, which nestles at the end of one of the state's most distinctively beautiful peninsulas. It is not surprising that Andrew Wyeth spent a lot of time painting here as well. On a clear day, the eleven-mile ride out to Monhegan is exhilarating.

In the days of commercial sail, vessels bearing Down East for northern European ports altered course at Monhegan, their last landfall, and checked their navigation before heading over the horizon. On the way back they steered for Newfoundland and then veered southeast along the North American coast. Monhegan is rich in seafaring history, both real and fancied, and there are periodic arguments over whether or not markings on a rock on nearby Manana Island, which with Monhegan forms Monhegan Harbor, are the work of ancient Phoenician mariners or just a whim of nature. In 1607, the *John and Mary* and the *Gift of God,* carrying emigrants for the short-lived Popham Colony, passed by Monhegan on the way to the mainland and stopped at the Georges Islands at the mouth of the St. George River, where they conducted a Church of England Mass. It was the first known English service of thanksgiving in New England, a historical footnote that later rankled the Puritan establishment in Massachusetts.

Well before permanent settlements were established on the mainland, Monhegan and other offshore islands were being used in summer by English fishermen to cure their catches before they set sail for the eastern Atlantic in the fall. Today the fishermen on Monhegan are year-round residents who do not range far from home. They stay close to the island, fishing for lobsters. Each year, to keep things equitable at sea and harmonious ashore, they haul all their traps as the year ends and reset them on New Year's Day, which on Monhegan is also called Trap Day. The idea is to prevent a monopoly of the fishing grounds by a few.

No cars are allowed on the island, whose village lanes can be congested with people in summer. Monhegan is a mile and a half long and half a mile wide, and has seventeen miles of hiking trails that run off from the village through pine forests. On the west side of the island, the trails weave beside the steep cliffs that make Monhegan a seamark. Offshore, yachtsmen use Monhegan to check their navigation, just as professional mariners did 150 years ago. Incoming freighters and oil tankers bound for Penobscot Bay ports pick up pilots off Monhegan, often on winter nights in rolling seas. And in August during the annual Monhegan Race—an overnighter from Portland—a large fleet of sleek racing yachts bears down on the island. To miss crowds, go in the spring or fall, or on a summer weekday.

Monhegan's beauty and the increase in the number of boats running to it have caused a summer influx of tourists, writers, and painters, augmenting the few families who have been summering here since before World War II. There is a museum at the base of Monhegan Island Light, and there is a chance of hiring a boat to get over to Manana.

When it is not foggy, the former Marshall Point Light station, with its walkway leading out to the light tower, is what you see from the deck of *Laura B* as it passes the easterly approach to Port Clyde Harbor on its way to and from Monhegan. The lighthouse is particularly noticeable on the way back. The station grounds are now a park, which has a broad view of the sea. The restored keeper's house is now a small but excellent museum devoted to St. George's past. The first light on the point was built in 1832. After subsequent renovations, the station was automated in 1980; in 1987 the Coast Guard leased it to the town of St. George, which turned the operation of the site over to the St. George Historical Society. There are signs in Port Clyde pointing the way to the station. It is not hard to find. Donations are encouraged, but admission is free.

Numerous artifacts and shell mounds left by Indians have been found on the St. George peninsula. The historical society likes to speculate that about 10,000 years ago the mysterious "Red Paint" people, whose burial sites span the North Atlantic but whose ethnic identity is only guessed at, may have been the region's first inhabitants. The original English settlers abandoned the peninsula during the French and Indian War. Resettlement by New Englanders began in 1763, after winning the war with the French who had claimed the St. George region, and the Indians who had been allied with them.

The first people to move onto the newly liberated peninsula were the descendants of Scots-Irish who in 1736 had settled Warren and Cushing (which then included St. George). By 1803, St. George had separated from Cushing, and General and Mrs. Knox became land managers for the new town, issuing deeds to established residents and selling unsettled land to others. For nearly the next hundred years, the residents set about farming, fishing, shipbuilding, granite quarrying, lumbering, cutting firewood for Thomaston limekilns and Boston fireplaces, and cutting ice for shipment to southern climes.

Between 1870 and 1930, there was an influx of Finnish, Swedish, Norwegian, Scottish, and English granite workers. Arriving with them by rail and steamship at Rockland was the first trickle of summer visitors, who, as their numbers increased and the local economy declined, began altering the tenor of the peninsula. The change is most noticeable at Tenants Harbor, which only twenty years ago was regarded as something of a placid paradise. It is now a tastefully crowded paradise for the combined reasons that it has long been a popular destination of cruising yachtsmen, because it is an easy harbor to make in most weather conditions, and because it is an easy drive from Thomaston and Rockland. Tenants Harbor is built up but remains one of the most softly beautiful locales on the coast, and it has inns and restaurants to match. If you want a quick lunch, AG Groceries has good take-out sandwiches.

State 131 and State 73 are well-paved country roads that meet at St. George, a village that has furnished live and still-life subjects for the Wyeths. It was also the scene of a British raid in which Capt. Samuel Watts, a Revolutionary and suspected smuggler, was captured and carried off to Castine. And it is the home of Robert Skoglund, The Humble Farmer, a humorist, a dispenser of local lore, a television and radio personality, and the host of a free picnic each summer. Skoglund has a sign in front of his house, and if he is not busy (he usually is), he sometimes talks with travelers about the region, particularly if they buy one of his videotapes about the Maine coast.

Fort St. Georges, near State 131 not far from the junction of State 73, was built on an island in the St. George River in 1809 during the clamor in Washington for a war with England. The War of 1812 came about, but no British troops came to attack Fort St. Georges. The fort is owned by the state but it is not maintained as a park and no signs point to it. Fort and island are accessible by boat; if you have a kayak or canoe strapped to your vehicle and can find a road that will take you within paddling distance of the island, it could be an interesting outing. There is no fee for visiting the fort.

Just north of St. George village on State 131 is a side road to Watts Point that passes by a historic cemetery beside a church. The cemetery is the more interesting of the two, and the road eventually becomes a gravel track leading toward the St. George River.

Heading east on State 73 from St. George, you come to Spruce Head and Spruce Head Island (accessible by causeway), which rival Tenants Harbor in beauty and a little in character. Spruce Head has managed to remain a vibrant lobster-fishing community. Fishing boats come and go here with dispatch. William Atwood and Sons, one of the state's major lobster dealers, arranges for the international shipment of lobsters from the company's pierside office. Each Christmas season, masses of Maine lobsters are air-freighted from Bangor International Airport to France and Belgium, where they are eaten on Christmas Eve. Other shipments are routinely made to the West Coast and Hawaii. Visible to the south from Spruce Head Island is Whitehead Island Light, at the southern end of Muscle Ridge Channel. Southeast is Two Bush Island Light, and beyond is the open sea.

If you are heading north on State 73 from South Thomaston, swing off in an easterly direction and tour the back roads leading to Ash Point, where there is a public beach, and to Owls Head village, where there is another public beach. Both communities are in the town of Owls Head, whose lobster-fishing fleets are being crowded by summer residences and the population spillover from Rockland, but for just driving or walking about, Owls Head village is a first-rate jaunt.

An interesting stop, if you are still on State 73, is the Owls Head Transportation Museum, which has a collection of what are known as landmark aircraft that the museum keeps in flying condition for air shows. The collection is the source of those World War I–vintage planes marked with German, British, and American insignias diving in mock combat above Owls Head and Penobscot Bay. A Peanuts cartoon fantasy by Snoopy come to life, the duels between Germany's Red Baron and one of Britain's

Sopwith Camels are reenacted here on lazy summer days. The museum's huge shed houses a collection of pioneer automobiles, engines, carriages, motorcycles, and bicycles. Antique and modern air shows, classic automobile shows, motorcycle meets, and truck and tractor meets attract 75,000 people annually. The museum is open year-round.

The north shore of Owls Head village forms the south end of Rockland Harbor. Owls Head Light stands on the peak of the headland, nearly a hundred feet above Penobscot Bay. From it is a superb view of the bay, taking in the Camden Hills and the large islands of Vinalhaven, Isle au Haut, North Haven, and Islesboro.

The Owls Head station, established in 1826, is surrounded now by a public park that is arranged for picnickers and nature walkers. A short stroll from the parking lot leads to the station, and a steep wooden stairway goes up to the white granite light tower, from which you can see Rockland Harbor and its light at the end of a mile-long granite breakwater. Below is the swirl of the current flowing around the headland and in and out of the northerly end of Muscle Ridge Channel. The state ferry to the offshore island of Matinicus passes by here. The abandoned range tower rising from a rock south of the light station marks the end of the measured mile that was used during U.S. Navy sea trials in the last century and the early part of this one to calculate the speed of newly built warships. The tower marking the other end of the measured mile, farther up the bay, was dismantled.

When passenger trains ran in Maine, Rockland was a distribution point for people bound for other places. Summer visitors from Boston, New York, and Philadelphia would ride the train to Rockland, where they would board steamships bound for Bar Harbor on Mount Desert Island and destinations in between. Today, Maine State ferries operating from the Rockland waterfront ply between the Penobscot Bay islands of North Haven and Vinalhaven and offshore to Matinicus, all excellent outings, if time permits.

If you are bound for North Haven or Matinicus, which are good-sized islands but walkable for people used to hiking, you can leave your vehicle in the parking lot beside the ferry terminal on the Rockland waterfront. None of these islands is as dramatically poised above the sea as Monhegan, but they are less crowded and the atmosphere ashore is generally more tranquil.

Before the Pilgrims landed in Plymouth, Capt. John Smith of Virginia was sending fishing schooners to Matinicus. One of the oldest settlements in the United States, Matinicus still has a plantation form of government and a culture peculiarly its own. Just south of Matinicus is Ragged Island, which once had a year-round fishing community but now has a seasonal one made up largely of fishermen from Rockland and summer residents. It was called Ragged Arse on eighteenth-century charts, but nineteenth-century chart makers in Washington deleted the second part of its name.

North Haven and Vinalhaven (once called the Fox Islands) are separated by Fox Islands Thorofare. Because they are less distant and more populous than Matinicus, ferries run to them with greater frequency. The North Haven ferry docks at the village, which consists mainly of Brown's boatyard, one of the oldest on the coast, a general store, a small restaurant, a yacht club, and an emporium of fine island crafts. This is the home of the North Haven dinghy, small, classically designed sailing craft that are raced in the annual North Haven Dinghy Race. There is a fishing fleet here, but in summer North Haven is a sanctuary for the rich, as is to a lesser degree Vinalhaven. If you are not a strong walker, bring your vehicle or a bicycle with you on the ferry, but you should know that the lanes on North Haven are more conducive to mountain bikes and horses than they are to modern automobiles. Probably the best form of transportation to bring would be a folding kayak. Once assembled, you could paddle it into the coves and inlets along Fox Islands Thorofare. There is a haul-out on the north shore of Vinalhaven, so you could explore two islands for the price of one ferry ticket. Other than the north

Lobster cars—wooden crates of live lobsters—off-loaded in Vinalhaven

shore of North Haven there are lots of places for paddlers to take shelter when the weather turns foul.

If you are afoot, North Haven's Pulpit Harbor, which is a slot in the island's north shore, is about an hour's walk from North Haven village. It is a beauty spot, popular among cruising yachtsmen, with a view of the Camden Hills in the distance. Mullen Head Park is on the east shore of the island and a much longer walk from the ferry landing. It faces East Penobscot Bay, providing distant views of Deer Isle and Isle au Haut and the smaller islands and headlands to the north. The park has campsites and is operated by the town of North Haven.

Vinalhaven is a much larger island with a different flavor. The ferry from Rockland puts in at Carvers Harbor on the southern end of the island, where the actual town of Vinalhaven is situated. Everything in the village is within walking distance of the harbor.

The town has a sturdy look, with a Civil War monument surrounded by a common, and a cluster of large, heavily timbered, nineteenth-century buildings that were erected along Main Street when the granite industry was flourishing. There are a few inns and motels, restaurants, food stores, a pharmacy, a fish processing plant that flash freezes lobsters for the export market, and the Vinalhaven Historical Society Museum, which displays a huge, horse-drawn wagon with twelve-foot-diameter wheels. Called a galamander and painted with the distinctive "Bodwell blue" of the Bodwell Granite Company, which operated on the island, it was used to haul large pieces of granite down Main Street to waiting schooners.

Granite was once a big business in Maine (the state was the nation's largest supplier of granite in 1901), and quarries were scattered along the coast from Wells to Calais, with the greatest number of them concentrated around Penobscot Bay. There were three quarries around Carvers Harbor, and the galamander was a familiar sight as it trundled along the streets of Vinalhaven. Skilled, itinerant workmen, many from the British Isles, blasted and drilled granite loose from the quarries in town and on Leadbetter, Gundelow, and Hurricane Islands off the west coast of Vinalhaven.

Across the bay on Deer Isle eight quarries were in operation. Granite from Vinalhaven, the St. George peninsula, and Deer Isle was shipped by sea and rail to help build the St. Lawrence Seaway, the Smithsonian Institution, the Library of Congress Annex, the U.S. Naval Academy, New York state's infamous Sing Sing Prison, New York City's main post office, the Cleveland and Chicago art museums, and numerous other post offices and government buildings throughout the nation.

On Vinalhaven immense pieces of granite were turned on huge lathes to carve the columns for New York City's St. John the Divine, the largest cathedral in North America. Polished watering troughs designed to slake the thirst of horses plying the nation's city streets and small town main streets were shipped from here along with hundreds of Civil War monuments and finely carved eagles and millions of paving blocks and flagstones. The dust and noise of quarrying did not cease in the region until 1930 when labor unrest and changes in architecture and materials, particularly the increasing use of concrete, finally took their toll.

There are three nature preserves on Vinalhaven, two within walking distance of the ferry slip. The third, Areys Neck Woods, is reachable on foot if you are a strong walker. Areys Neck is located on the east side of the island facing Isle au Haut (pronounced locally as "aisle a Ho" and "aisle a Holt"). A trail leads from a parking area through a spruce wood beside Arey Cove and over a hill to a marsh.

Armbrust Hill Wildlife Reservation, on the edge of the harbor, is the site of a former granite quarry and has trails leading by a small pond, stands of birches, scenic overlooks, what is known as a quarry garden, and spots for picnicking. Lanes Island Preserve, accessible by causeway, has a rock-strewn shore and an interior patchwork of blueberry, rose, and bayberry bushes, spruce trees, and rolling, variegated moors.

Rockland proclaims itself the Lobster Capital of the World, which may be a little exaggerated, and the Schooner Capital of Maine, which may be an understatement. The city's motto is "God Gives a Reward to Industry." The nerve center of that industry remains in the banks, law offices, and shops that are housed in the red-brick and granite-trimmed Greek Revival, Italianate, and Colonial Revival buildings that face each other along Rockland's Main Street Historic District.

The district is included in a walking tour (Harbor Walk) that meanders from a boat launching ramp and the Outward

Friendship sloops off Rockland Harbor Light

Bound Survival School headquarters at the south end of the harbor to the Maine State Ferry Service terminal near the harbor's north end. It is a long walk (Rockland Harbor is one of the biggest in the state), but because the Harbor Walk is along city streets, there is the option of driving it. A Chamber of Commerce office at Harbor Park on the waterfront provides Harbor Walk maps and information on almost anything you want to know about Rockland, including a variety of boat rides. If you are coming into town on State 73 (South Main Street) from Owl's Head, turn right onto Mechanic Street and follow the harbor, turning left onto Atlantic Street and then, always bearing right, continue on a series of short streets to Harbor Park. You will have already driven the first third of the Harbor Walk. If that is more than you want to try, just look for signs pointing to the waterfront when you get into town. Driving in Rockland can be problematic, because Main Street is one way, headed north, and if you miss a turn you can wind up exploring more of the city than you intended.

In early July, Harbor Park is where the action is after the Annual Great Schooner Race, which starts from North Haven in the morning and ends at the entrance to Rockland Harbor in the afternoon. Sails and rigging pop and crackle in the wind as large schooners, ketches, and brigantines round into the harbor and pass the park in a sail-by before lying to beside the park and the Black Pearl Restaurant, which sits out from the park on pilings rising from the harbor. The postrace awards ceremony is preceded and followed by the rhythmic, reedy lilt of sea chanties sung by good and not-so-good folksingers. It is a public party, often accompanied by dancing, that goes on into the evening.

In early August, the park is the center of activity for the three-day Annual Maine Lobster Festival, and there are lobsters galore.

Rockland is a city with a very salty past. In November 1853, *Red Jacket,* an elegantly appointed, record-breaking, extreme clipper of 2,306 tons, was launched from the George Thomas Shipyard on Rockland's waterfront and became one of Maine's most world famous if not its most famous sailing vessel. She made her maiden voyage from New York to Liverpool in January 1854 in thirteen days, one hour, and twenty-five minutes, and rounded into the dock at Liverpool under full sail. Almost before her lines were made fast to the wharf, England's White Star Line, which later changed its name after its liner *Titanic* sank, chartered *Red Jacket* and put her on the Australia run, where she set another record. Shortly after *Red Jacket* was launched, Rockland's Merriam Shipyard sent *Euterpe* down the ways. She made a record-breaking run from Calcutta, round Cape Horn, to London in eighty-five days.

It was during this era that Rockland's marine artist James G. Babbidge began going to sea. Most of Babbidge's ship portraits are in private collections, but his earliest known painting hangs in the Mariner's Museum in Newport News, Virginia, and his last known work is displayed at the Mystic (Connecticut) Seaport Museum.

Babbidge and two other Penobscot Bay marine artists of the same period, Percy A. Sanborn of Belfast and William P. Stubbs of Bucksport, were born in the 1840s, when Maine was approaching the pinnacle of its shipbuilding prosperity. Their paintings are periodically grouped together during special marine shows at the Farnsworth Art Museum, located at Elm and Museum Streets in downtown Rockland, which displays among other things a collection of paintings, sculptures, collages, and designs by Rockland-raised artist Louise Nevelson.

The Farnsworth is open year-round, and its Main Street entry can be one of the more rewarding places to duck into during a rain squall. The museum complex has a permanent exhibit of major American artists who have painted in Maine: Fitz Hugh Lane, Jonathan Fisher, Winslow Homer, Marsden Hartley, Edward Hopper, Rockwell Kent, the Wyeths, and Neil Welliver. Their works are in the museum's original building at Elm and Museum. Around the corner on Elm Street is the 1850 Greek Revival Farnsworth Homestead, open from June through September and designed to show how a successful, nineteenth-century Rockland merchant family lived.

Shore Village Museum, Rockland's other museum, has little to do with fine art and a lot to do with lighthouses and the sea. Run by retired career coastguardsman Ken Black, who has done lighthouse duty and served on lightships, Shore Village has the largest collection of lighthouse and Coast Guard memorabilia on display in the nation. Inside the Victorian house the museum occupies at 104 Limerock Street is a huge Fresnel lens, fabricated in 1855 for Petit Manan Light Station, which has the highest light tower on the Maine coast. The history of lighthouses, particularly Maine lighthouses and lifesaving stations, is all here. This is a museum made unique by the scope of its presentation and the dedication of its curator, who has wrung more saltwater out of his socks than most people see in a lifetime.

Rockland Harbor's north end is the home of most of the city's schooner fleet, which, with vessels in other Penobscot Bay ports, makes up the largest collection of traditional, commercial sailing craft in the country. Two of these Rockland vessels, the handsomely restored schooners *Lewis R. French* and *Mercantile*, once carried kilnwood and lime for Rockland's lime trade. Raw material (limerock) from the surface of Rockland's lime beds was trundled over to the waterfront brick kilns where the heat from wood fires turned it into lime (calcium oxide), used to make mortar and cement. The kilns were located at the base of cliffs, so limerock could be dumped in from above, fires stoked from below, and the finished product extracted at pier level and wheeled into the holds of waiting ships. Smoke billowed night and day from the fires of forty-seven limekilns. Mariners entering Rockland Harbor at night to deliver firewood and take on lime were greeted by a crescent of flickering flames that shimmered across the water.

6
Rockport and Camden

Between US 1 and Penobscot Bay, the residential districts of Rockport and Camden flow together along tree-shadowed roads winding through woods and pastures. This bulge of land between Camden and Rockport, which once were one community, is still a backwater where the drone of bees is contrapuntal to the rush of summer traffic along US 1. The landscape is well-kempt, the houses are shipshape, and brown-and-white Belted Galloway cattle munch lush grass in a setting as serene as an early-nineteenth-century oil depicting the virtues of country life.

If you instead happen to be taking the shorter way between Rockport and Camden, US 1, there is respite from it at the end of Conway Road—the sixty-six-acre nature park called Merryspring, which sprawls over the Camden-Rockport town line. Merryspring is open to the public year-round from sunrise to sunset, with no admission fee. Marked trails lead through meadows and woods and beside wildflowers and shrubs. In summer, horticulturists deliver lectures from the park's gazebo on almost everything you need to know about gardening. The small, hand-lettered sign for Merryspring is on the west side of US 1. On the way to the park is the Conway House and Cramer Museum, which recreate how life was lived in the region in the 1700s.

Of the two downtowns, Rockport's, built on the side of a hill that plummets to the harbor, is the most charmingly picturesque, which is probably why a national photography school, The Maine

Photographic Workshops, is located there—along the curve of Main Street near Mary Lea Park, overlooking the harbor. Nearly opposite the photography school is a coffee and sandwich shop, and down and around the corner from it, along a sidewalk with an iron rail, are a few antiques shops. Up Main Street in the opposite direction is the 1891 Opera House, whose interior with its flying balcony is one of the most visually pleasing sights in town, other than the harbor. Bay Chamber Concerts has performances here in winter and summer. The Rockport Historical Society has an office in the Opera House. It is well worth the inquiry to take a look inside even if the Bay Chamber Concerts' schedule does not suit you.

Farther uphill around a curve to the right, inside a refurbished livery stable, is the Maine Coast Artists gallery. The interior of the stable building and the views of foliage and flower beds from its windows are almost as interesting as the paintings and sculptures.

Almost opposite the coffee and sandwich shop is a dead-end road leading down to the harbor and to a boatyard. On the left just before the boatyard is the Sail Loft restaurant, whose dining room has an excellent harbor view, as well as good food, and is open year round.

The Goose River, which empties into the head of the harbor through a gorge, has cut the village into two sections, connected by a bridge. Upriver from the bridge is an old mill dam; at the south end of the bridge is Marine Park, a broad expanse of grass behind which historic limekilns are set in a steep, wooded hillside. At the end of the line of kilns, Goose River (Rockport's old name) floods into the V-shaped harbor, where the schooner *Timberwind* takes on summer passengers for cruises on the bay. Here also is a polished granite statue of Andre, a foundling seal pup who was adopted by a Rockport resident and soon became something of a community pet. Andre has been the subject of numerous New England newspaper articles and two books, *A Seal Called Andre* and *Andre,* a children's book that captured the fancy of young readers across the nation.

Several hundred yards beyond the *Timberwind* dock is the large, heavily timbered shed of the Artisans School, a boatbuilding school specializing in traditional designs. It is a fascinating place, and visitors are welcome to watch wooden boats being built, or examine finished ones on display, seven days a week. The school is off Elm Street on Sea Street a short distance from Marine Park and on the way to a third park, Walker Park, which also has a harbor view and is set up for picnics and cookouts.

The limekilns at Marine Park were once part of an industry that began in the early nineteenth century. Lime to mix cement for the construction of the nation's Capitol was shipped from the Goose River (Rockport) section of Camden. In the hundred years of its existence, the lime industry employed thousands of kiln workers, quarrymen, coopers, teamsters, and mariners. Money from the lime trade and shipbuilding built much of Rockport, including its opera house.

Kiln fires burned round the clock while the ships of Rockport's lime fleet were being loaded for the community's major market of Boston and its lesser markets of Portland, Wilmington, Charleston, and Jacksonville. On their return passage the lime ships brought back merchandise for local retailers who not uncommonly were, like the shipbuilders, major investors in the lime industry. The kiln fires were stoked with locally cut cordwood from the interior and as far up the bay as Sears Island, where a floating sawmill had been moored. By the end of the nineteenth century, cordwood was being shipped from New Brunswick and Nova Scotia, in stubby, two-masted vessels built along the Bay of Fundy that came to be a common sight along the Maine coast and were known as "Johnny Woodboats," or sometimes just "Johnny Bull boats," because Canada was still governed by England and John Bull was the cartoon personification of England as Uncle Sam was of the United States.

The waning of the hurly-burly of industrial activity in Rockport and Camden roughly coincided with the construction of a Victorian resort hotel at scenic Jameson Point in Rockport's otherwise drab section of Glen Cove, just over the Rockland city line. The old hotel burned, and the modern wood, stone, and glass Samoset Resort now stands over the original foundation. The Samoset's golf course is laid out along the edge of Penobscot Bay, and there are sweeping views of the bay from the Samoset's lobby, dining room, and terrace. Where the resort's property ends on the north side of Rockland Harbor is a footpath to the breakwater, a popular spot from which to watch the annual Great Schooner Race, or to just have a picnic. The mile-long, granite-block structure runs from the shore to Rockland Breakwater Light.

Camden looks like a crowded movie set in summer; and it was the setting for the films *Peyton Place, Carousel,* and the remake of *Captains Courageous.*

Camden has a large private fleet, boat rentals, and a sizable fleet of passenger schooners, which are available for week-long or day cruises. Some of the charter vessels once hauled lime, granite, Christmas trees, fish, and cordwood from Maine ports to points along the East Coast. Now immaculately restored, they and newer schooners and their crews wait between excursions beside the Camden waterfront, which is often thronged with people milling between the downtown shops, the vessels, and nearby waterside restaurants. The Camden Chamber of Commerce maintains an information booth on the waterfront.

From June through September, there can be from six to eight classic, gaff-rigged schooners tied up in Camden Harbor. Their stout, oiled masts and spiderwebs of tarred rigging rise above the bowl of the upper harbor, which is bordered by well-landscaped Harbor Park, a popular spot for picnicking and boat watching. North of the park and across a small stream is the boatbuilding and boat brokerage complex of Wayfarer Marine. Behind the park are the Camden Public Library and the Camden Amphitheatre, where arts and crafts are displayed in summer. Looming inland from the park is Mount Battie, which inspired Pulitzer Prize–winning poet Edna St. Vincent Millay to write, "I'm nobody. Who are you?" as she gazed from the height at the blue vastness of Penobscot Bay and the Gulf of Maine. There is a plaque in her honor on the summit of Mount Battie and a statue of her in Harbor Park. The public library has two scrapbooks of Millay memorabilia.

South of Harbor Park and next to it is a torrent of water rushing down the spillway of an old mill dam. It is refreshingly pleasant, and when you are beside it watching the white water cascade toward the harbor it is easy to forget that only a few feet away is US 1 (Main Street). Just down Main Street from the spillway is the Camden Deli, which serves good food on its enclosed porch overlooking the cascade and the harbor.

Camden's Main Street is a neatly kept midway of gift, jewelry, and antiques shops and good places to eat. More downtown shops and restaurants are along Bayview Street, which runs off Main Street and follows the south side of the harbor, and along the alleys running from Bayview Street down to the harbor itself. Bayview Street eventually passes by the Camden Harbor Inn, expensive but excellent food and view, and then the Camden Yacht Club and Ogier Point, where the road begins a ramble in the direction of Rockport.

Not long before the American Revolution, Camden had developed into a small community with a sawmill, a gristmill, about ten houses, and, later, as it turned out, a population with a fair number of people with revolutionary tendencies. At least merchants in Castine across the bay felt so and sent a deputation to Halifax, Nova Scotia, to ask that a British garrison be sent to the region to protect Castine's fledgling shipping interests from the Camden radicals. The British complied and began a generally successful hounding of the region's rebels in what amounted to a mishmash of minor raids and skirmishes. These were not great moments in the annals of British and American arms, but they did place Camden, Rockport, and Rockport's Glen Cove section in footnotes to the American Revolution.

After the British burned ordnance stores at Camden, American reinforcements were sent up the bay in five whaleboats

Windjammers in Camden Harbor

and captured two British schooners, taking them to Glen Cove. Pursuing British vessels tacked back and forth in Glen Cove, assessing the situation while the American militia gathered along the shore where one of the captured British vessels had been hauled out, the other captured schooner having escaped to seaward. After several hours the British apparently decided a fight was not worth the cannons aboard the schooner and sailed back to Castine with only an extended day sail to show for their effort. The Americans took the cannons to Thomaston.

Camden was incorporated in 1791, named by its citizenry for Charles Pratt, the first earl of Camden, who as a member of the British House of Lords had opposed the Stamp Act and in so doing made Camden a popular name in the Colonies. By the nineteenth century, Camden Harbor had become a major Maine shipbuilding center and a minor mill town. By midcentury, Camden had lost its bid to be the Knox County shiretown to more politically and financially powerful Rockland, and in so doing became destined to remain a quiet community.

At about the same time that Rockland was celebrating becoming a beehive of a county capital and Camden was resigning itself to being quietly picturesque, a trickle of summer residents from the lumber-rich, bustling Penobscot River city of Bangor began to appear in Camden. Eventually a great number of Philadelphians helped create a turn-of-the-century real estate boom of summer cottages that spilled over into Rockport.

Camden has been slowly reverting to being a year-round community. It now has a small publishing, graphics, and advertising industry, and its former mill buildings, set back from the water in a web of streets behind Main Street have been converted into thriving minimalls and commercial offices. One sprawling old mill complex that has been spiffily renovated now houses an international computer network system used by major credit card companies. After more than a hundred years since losing its chance to be the county's shiretown, Camden has leaped ahead of

Rockland from its newly formed economic base. It remains one of the few year-round recreational communities on the coast.

The Camden Snow Bowl (downhill and cross-country skiing) is outside of town at 1,300-foot-high Ragged Mountain, whose slopes look down on Hosmer Pond—the source of the Goose River—and the sweep of Penobscot Bay and the Gulf of Maine. The Snow Bowl has nine downhill trails, snowmaking machines, chairlifts, T-bars, and a 400-foot toboggan chute, the only public one in the state. There is ice skating on Hosmer Pond and in summer the Snow Bowl offers tennis and canoeing.

Leaving downtown Camden, US 1 swings from Main Street to High Street and into what seems like a mile-long succession of well-landscaped, beautifully maintained houses. As motel signs come into view at the left bend in the road, there is a "Maine Coon Cat" sign on the right behind some trees and a stockade fence. The cattery is open by appointment and by chance. It specializes in Maine coon cats, those large, fluffy, often ring-tailed, six-toed descendants of Norwegian forest cats that once were a common sight in Maine.

About a mile down the road from the cattery is the entrance to Camden Hills State Park, which sprawls over a tract between Penobscot Bay and Lake Megunticook. The park is almost the same size as Camden and Rockport proper combined. A network of trails takes hikers, cross-country skiiers, and snowmobilers up, down, and around Mount Battie, Mount Megunticook, and Bald Rock Mountain, all of which have excellent views of Penobscot Bay. If time is short or you do not feel like hiking, there is a toll road to the top of Mount Battie, where a round stone observation tower has been built. It is a short walk from the parking lot to the panoramic view at the edge of the summit, and only about a thirty-foot climb up a stone staircase to the tower's open observation deck. From behind its stone parapet you can look directly down on Camden Harbor, and then off in the rich blue distance to the forested islands of the bay.

7
Islesboro, Belfast, Searsport, and Stockton Springs

The best way to get a quick fix on this region of upper Penobscot Bay is to charter a sight-seeing plane at Belfast Airport, which is not as expensive a ride as you might think.

The best way to begin a tour of the region is to take the ferry from Lincolnville to Islesboro, a serene island in the middle of upper Penobscot Bay, still sometimes called by its old name of Long Island.

Lincolnville is a small bayside village flanking US 1. Cordwood was once loaded here to be taken to the limekilns in Camden, Rockport, and Rockland. Nineteenth-century mariners' houses are clustered on either side of the village, whose shops face Ducktrap Beach. The slightly ramshackle storefronts may look like a cartoon of summertime in New England come to life, but the beach is a good one despite its proximity to US 1, and the views from it of Ducktrap Harbor to the north and easterly to Islesboro are worth a stop. Just north of the beach, which is popular with windsurfers, are two shoreside restaurants. The ferry terminal and its parking lot are just south of the beach.

Looking astern over the wake of the ferry *Margaret Chase Smith* (named for one of Maine's most popular U.S. senators) as it churns its way to Islesboro, the Camden Hills loom above the bay like a line of huge, colossally rumpled, bluish green pillows strewn in the direction of Rockland. To the north is Belfast Bay and the far outline of Searsport, where oceangoing cargo vessels call. Forward, looking from the ferry's promenade decks, sunlight flashes on the lantern room windows of Grindle Point Light, just above the Islesboro ferry landing.

Grindle Point is on the north side of the entrance to Gilkey Harbor, which is ringed with large summer houses and is named for John Gilkey, who came to the island in 1772. In the early part of this century, Islesboro was a summer resort in the grand manner, and yachts such as J. P. Morgan's *Corsair* (built at Bath Iron Works in Bath) could be seen riding at anchor in the harbor. On the south side of the harbor entrance is spruce-covered Warren Island, where there is a state park accessible only by boat. The island's main village, Dark Harbor, is located on the east side of Gilkey Harbor. The village and its namesake boatyard lent their name to a lovely little gaff-rigged sailer, the Dark Harbor 17, which used to be a common sight in the region.

Grindle Point is named for Francis Grindle, who sold three acres of his land to the government in the 1840s to build a light station. The U.S. Lighthouse Service put up twenty-nine light stations along the Maine coast between 1820 and 1852, a period of burgeoning commercial shipping activity on Penobscot Bay, when independent shipping lines were linking its ports with the world and passenger steamship lines were linking Maine with the rest of New England. During the nineteenth century the largest commercial shipping fleet in the bay, the Pendleton fleet, was based at Islesboro. In the 1930s, the Grindle Point Light was automated and the station was sold to the town of Islesboro, which turned the station into a park and the keeper's house into what is now the Sailor's Memorial Museum. The Coast Guard continues to maintain the automated, white-flashing light atop a twenty-one-foot-high, skeletal steel tower on the seaward side of the former light station.

Driving around Islesboro, or more literally driving up and down it, is probably more interesting if you are a photographer or a painter, because most of the views of the bay are tree limb–filtered vistas, except at Dark Harbor village and Pendleton Point, at the south end of the island. Islesboro is a long, narrow island that lies roughly on a north-south axis. There is a small fishing fleet and there are a few residents who commute to jobs on the mainland, but much of the income of the year-round population is derived in some way from seasonal residency.

Back on the mainland north of the ferry landing, the Ducktrap area, which follows the contours of Ducktrap Harbor, is one of the most visually pleasing sections of US 1 in Waldo County. The name "Ducktrap" comes from the colonial practice of slaughtering migrating ducks en masse in the fall as a hedge against winter hunger. If you like smoked salmon and smoked sea trout, find the Pitcher Pond Road on the Lincolnville side of Ducktrap and head for Ducktrap River Fish Farms, Inc.

Farther up the coast in Northport, US 1 begins to bend away from the bay on its course toward Belfast, in effect dropping an obscuring curtain of vegetation between the highway and the bay. Near the village of Northport, the Shore Road will lead you down to the water. It is a secondary road best avoided in winter and particularly during spring thaws, but otherwise the views make it worth taking.

At its Northport end, Shore Road drops down beside Saturday Cove and then meanders along the bay for a few miles before coming to Temple Heights, a Spiritualist colony facing the north end of Islesboro across West Penobscot Bay. Serious mediums perform serious seances here, and if you are a Spiritualist or profess an interest in Spiritualism you can probably rent a room. They are available. A few miles beyond Temple Heights is South Shore Boat, which builds a comely day sailer as well as Down East–style fishing boats and yachts designed by Calvin Beal, Jr., of Beals Island. South Shore does not always have a sign out, so if you want to take a look at what they do, you might have to ask around.

Farther up the Shore Road is Bayside, a collection of gingerbread, turn-of-the-century cottages built on the site of a nineteenth-century Methodist campground. The cottages rise where tents were once pitched by the ancestors of some of today's cottage owners. The gingerbread cottages sit eave by eave along narrow, tree-shaded dirt lanes that run downhill to a large, private community park by the bay. The small building by the pier at the bottom of the sloping park is the local yacht club, which is private. The large, rambling building at the upper end of the park is the community building, which is also private. That may seem like a lot of privacy, but the local residents do not seem to mind visitors, as long as the tranquillity of the place is not disturbed. Nearby is the Northport golf course, which is public.

The Shore Road rejoins US 1 in East Northport, where there is the surprise of seeing a brightly painted Mexican restaurant, Dos Amigos. The restaurant must have something going for it, because it has been there a long time.

Farther north on US 1 is Belfast, a city whose old district was fortunate enough to have been bypassed by the highway. It has been left as something of a time capsule of distinquished buildings that have only recently begun to be popularly appreciated. Along High Street and Court Street are some of the best examples of Greek Revival, Federal, and Victorian houses in the state, all a legacy of Belfast's prosperous nineteenth-century maritime activity, when hundreds of first-class vessels were launched from shipyards along the city's waterfront. Belfast's original downtown commercial buildings, which were constructed of wood, were destroyed by fire. Their taller, more stately successors, rendered in decorative brickwork by nineteenth-century masons, stand as a testament to past craftsmanship.

Belfast was established in the late 1760s by a group of developers from Londonderry, New Hampshire, who had the site for their maritime city surveyed and built to plan. Most of the streets are at right angles to each other, and the spacing between them was designed to allow as many views of the bay as possible, a thoughtfulness that is still in evidence. During the Revolution and the War of 1812, Belfast was taken by the British but never occupied, probably because it was a short sail across the bay from their garrison in Castine. At City Hall on Church Street, you can pick up a guide to Belfast, which includes an all-too-brief history of the city but a very adequate street map and list of historic places. On Market Street, just around a corner from City Hall, is the local historical museum.

Main Street, the central corridor of commercial activity, runs downhill to Belfast Harbor from the intersection with Church Street at historic Post Office Square. The dominant building in Post Office Square is, appropriately, the 1855 Italianate Post Office/Customs House, from whose steps you can look down Main Street to the sparkling surface of the water just off the City Landing. In the nineteenth century, several thousand commercial vessels a year sailed in and out of these waters, making Penobscot Bay the most heavily trafficked region in the state. Structures built during Belfast's maritime prosperity include the Victorian Gothic former Belfast National Bank building and the transitional Greek Revival Italianate Hayford Block, which contains the Opera House. The Opera House, which is still used by local theatrical troupes, is being refurbished.

Today, commercial carriers are outnumbered by pleasure craft and fishing vessels, but the bay is still Maine's heaviest traffic area for commercial shipping by volume of cargo imported to and exported from the state. Foreign-flag vessels calling at Searsport and Bucksport are monitored by U.S. Customs and Coast Guard personnel from their offices on the second floor of the Post Office/Customs House. The Penobscot Bay Pilots Association is based here. Most of its licensed captains who conn vessels in and out of the bay are graduates of Maine Maritime Academy in Castine, across the bay. Also based here is the regional chapter of the Propeller Club, a national maritime lobbying group whose members come from all over midcoast and Down East Maine. There are no signs proclaiming these organizations, but it is interesting to know that Belfast still has associations with the working maritime world beneath the growing overlay of interesting art galleries and cafes dotting Main and High Streets and numerous bed and breakfasts in the old residential district.

Belfast has come a long way from the 1970s, when feathers from chicken processing plants along the waterfront swirled in the wind of lower Main Street. The feathers have gone along with the chicken plants, and a waterfront park with picnic tables now covers the slope near the City Landing where the processing plants stood. Because it has cleaned itself up, Belfast is now an increasingly popular summer anchorage with yachtsmen. There is a large seafood restaurant and a good fast-food booth next to the City Landing. Just up the Passagassawakeag River, which flows into the harbor, is Marshall Wharf, where Maineport Towing, Inc., keeps its oceangoing tugs tethered. The tugs surge in and out of Belfast Bay on their way to dock and undock freighters and tankers at Searsport and Bucksport. Next to Marshall Wharf is Belfast Boat Yard. On its landward side is a terminus of the Belfast & Moosehead Railroad, which offers excursion rides into the interior.

In East Belfast, on the other side of the Passagassawakeag River on US 1/State 3, is one of the state's first-rate boatbuilders, Holland Boat Shop, located on Mill Lane. Holland Boat builds graceful, fiberglass fishing boats and yachts. In the 1970s and 1980s, Holland earned fame on the lobster boat racing circuit with its souped-up speedster *Red Baron,* which ran repeated duels with the Young Brothers' *Sopwith Camel* as the two builders vied for a bigger share of the Maine fishing boat market. Today *Red Baron* is moored in Belfast Harbor and is used as a pilot boat.

Also in East Belfast, on Mitchell Avenue, is Young's Lobster Pound, which has a good view of the harbor and the bay and specializes in shore dinners. Perry's Tropical Nut House, on US 1/State 3, has a large display of what its sign suggests.

Just over the East Belfast line in Searsport is Moose Point State Park, with picnic tables, bayside trails, and good views that

Brick Victorians in downtown Searsport along US 1

sometimes include cargo ships anchored offshore waiting to get into Searsport. In summer huge Military Sealift Command vessels attached to the nation's Rapid Deployment Force anchor off here to escape the heat of southern East Coast ports while they await assignment to world trouble spots.

Searsport has a rich maritime past that is often used as an example of coastal village life in the nineteenth century. In 1860, one-fifth of Maine's male population was merchant mariners; in Searsport, whose population was just under 2,000, the percentage of mariners was much higher. By the 1870s and 1880s, 10 percent of the shipmasters in the U.S. Merchant Marine used Searsport as their hailing port. Their vessels, which they sailed to the major ports of the world, were built at the head of the harbor. Later as larger vessels were needed, Searsport's mariners turned to shipyards in the deeper water ports of Bangor, Brewer, Bath, Newcastle, and Damariscotta.

If you look sharp while driving through town on US 1/State 3, you will see a sign pointing to the town landing, from which there are good views of the harbor, the point where the port is, and upper Penobscot Bay. Searsport abounds in houses facing the bay that were built by local sailors, gone to rest long ago in Bowditch Cemetery, where no Bowditch is buried. The cemetery is named for Nathaniel Bowditch, author of *American Practical Navigator—An Epitome of Navigation and Nautical Astronomy,* which contained the first set of accurate navigational tables published in the nation. According to local lore, the mariners who began the cemetery in the 1850s decided to name it Bowditch under the theory that having steered them well in life, Bowditch might be a help in navigating their course in the afterlife.

Their story and Penobscot Bay's story is displayed in the Penobscot Marine Museum complex, which occupies a restored district of Searsport's downtown tucked away off US 1/State 3. Marine paintings by nineteenth-century Chinese and European artists of Penobscot Bay vessels at various ports of call hang in the museum's buildings, which surround the First Congregational Church. The works of marine artists Thomas and James Buttersworth are displayed in a gallery named for them, and works by Bucksport's native son William Pierce Stubbs as well as Antonio Jacobsen are prominent on the museum's walls. The admission fee for the entire complex is less than the price of a movie, and you can stay there all day, which makes it a most pleasing way to absorb Penobscot Bay's maritime culture. In summer the museum has a festival that includes a rendezvous of classically designed sailing vessels off the Town Landing. In keeping with the town's maritime heritage, Otis Enterprise Marine Corporation, on Prospect Street, builds work and pleasure boats, which are shipped up and down the East Coast and to the Great Lakes.

Toward the end of the last century, a different type of boat was built here. It was the yacht *Defender,* which in 1895, with a large number of Maine sailors aboard, bested *Valkyrie III,* the British challenger for the America's Cup. *Defender* sailed for the New York Yacht Club in one of the more rancorous cup defenses on record.

Searsport is also the birthplace of the man who wrote the lyrics for the University of Maine's "Stein Song," which in 1930 Maine crooner Rudy Vallee made the nation's number one hit. Lincoln Colcord, who was reared and educated aboard his parents' ship before entering the class of 1904 at the University of Maine, wrote the words for the "Stein Song" while he was an undergraduate.

On the east side of Searsport, US 1/State 3 swings through a cluster of large Victorian sea captains' houses that are now bed and breakfasts and antiques shops. One of these was once the summer residence of Bangor artist Waldo Peirce, who hung around with Ernest Hemingway in Paris in the 1920s and 1930s. Beyond is a cluster of outdoor flea markets and then Hamilton Marine, the largest marine supply retailer east of Boston. Hamilton Marine is a favorite with boatbuilders, commercial fishermen, and serious yachtsmen.

The side road beside Hamilton Marine leads to the port at Mack Point from which munitions were shipped to Great Britain during World Wars I and II. Indians in cargo canoes used Mack Point in their coastal trade before the white man came. During World War I, two large piers and a railhead were constructed at Mack Point to transport munitions across the Atlantic. The reasoning was Maine ports are the nearest ones in the United States to Europe and a munitions train blowing up in sparsely populated Maine would do less damage to the war effort than it would if it exploded in Boston. During both wars feeder convoys, destined for the North Atlantic run, were assembled off Searsport and Stockton Springs. The feeder convoys would steam for Halifax, Nova Scotia, or Point Judith, Rhode Island, where they joined the main convoys. During World War II, German U-boats prowled

the Gulf of Maine, and survivors of the convoy runs recall seeing
vessels blown into fireballs before they reached Halifax or Point
Judith. The port administrators do not encourage visitors,
because the heavy equipment in motion around the piers is dangerous to the unwary. You can get a fairly good look at Mack
Point about a mile or so farther down US 1/State 3 from Hamilton
Marine, or a better one from Sears Island.

Despite being in a heavy industry zone, Sears Island, just
ahead on US 1/State 3, has been and remains a locally popular
recreation spot for those who know how to find the access road
(near the Searsport–Stockton Springs line). The island is a favorite
with hikers, swimmers, cross-country skiers, and picnickers. Parts
of the island have been designated by the state as wildlife sanctuaries. The island, with Cape Jellison in Stockton Springs, forms
Stockton Harbor, which in the last century was alive with shipping
and shipbuilding activity.

Stockton Springs adopted its present name in an ill-fated
attempt to market mineral water when its maritime economic base
began to fail. The village's small commercial district, just off
US 1/State 3, has a semiabandoned look to it most of the year, but
it is on the way to Fort Pownal State Park, which merits a visit.

The park is at the end of a finger of land extending from Cape
Jellison. Fort Pownal, now a ruin, was once the most easterly outpost of the English in North America. This is where the Penobscot
River begins to widen into Penobscot Bay, and from their vantage
point on Cape Jellison the English kept an eye on what the French
were doing across the river in Old Acadia. The park abuts Fort
Point Light, which is maintained by the Coast Guard. It is the light
you see gleaming in the distance from the opposite side of the bay
as you drive down to Castine in the evening. The light warns vessels of an offshore ledge, which has a day mark atop a stone monument on it for good measure. From the Castine Road, when the
tide is out, the monument resembles a surfaced submarine. The
park and rural, residential Cape Jellison are worth rambling about.

8

Gateway: Bucksport, Bangor, and Winterport

Real Down East Maine begins at the Penobscot River, and the gateways to it are through Bucksport and Bangor. The two communities are linked by history and the river, which just below Bucksport flows into Penobscot Bay, the state's largest estuary. If you are driving along the coast, Bucksport is the obvious and the most convenient gateway.

But Bangor has a centuries-old lure. And for those driving rental cars away from Bangor International Airport, or who are approaching from the Maine Turnpike, Bangor is a gateway to Down East. It is a city more associated with woods than the water, but it is nonetheless a city with a maritime past and that boasts being once the lumber port of the world.

Most people would happily put both communities in their wakes as rapidly as possible during summer heat waves, but the Penobscot River valley between Bangor and Bucksport is worth a look for its history, its isolated spots of charm, and its general beauty. The Penobscot River has given the area its life and its romance. It rises in interior Maine near Jackman by the Quebec border and flows through what was once one of the richest timbered areas in the world before reaching Bangor.

It was at Bucksport that Bangor-bound sailing vessels would gather after spring ice-out to be towed upriver by steam-driven tugboats. The waiting vessels would moor out of the main stream between the waterfront and Verona Island, where today pleasure boats and the town's few remaining fishing vessels moor. Before steam-powered towboats, the lumber schooners carried sturdy pulling boats, known as yawl boats, which were powered by oar-wielding sailors. When there was no wind, or when the wind was not blowing the right way, yawl boats and sailors were lowered over the side for what was a long pull upriver to the world's lumber capital.

Bucksport today has something of a split personality. It is a community that has had the contours of a mill town grafted onto its lumber, shipbuilding, and fishing foundation. The incision scars run along Main Street, where the mill economy and the automobile have swept away most traces of the town's nineteenth-century maritime economy and culture. Major oceangoing vessels, mostly oil tankers from Europe, Asia, Africa, and Central America, unload cargo here while off-duty crewmen shop ashore.

Champion International Corporation owns the large blue and white utilitarian complex on the river in Bucksport. The paper mill runs round the clock. White vapor drifts skyward from the mill's massive emission stack. The huge hill of pulpwood is used to make high-quality, lightweight paper for magazines. In summer the mill has regular tour schedules. If it is off-season, ask about a tour at the information office inside the main gate.

The Champion mill is on a site occupied in previous centuries by a foundry and tanneries. Before that, Indians gathered grasses here to make baskets, and salmon were once caught here as they made their annual spring run to the head of the tide at Bangor and the freshwater spawning grounds above the Bangor falls.

Bucksport's restaurants all seem to be located on Main Street, and all of them are good, including the take-out ice-cream shop, The Dairy Port. (Crosby's, the other ice-cream shop, is on the way to the Bucksport Public Golf Course, on State 46.) The best river view from any in-town restaurant is from the dining room of the Dockside Restaurant, whose windows face the Bucksport Town Wharf and Fort Knox. It is a good place for breakfast. The food is simple and good but not designed for dieters.

For atmosphere but not much view, try MacLeod's, Jed Prouty's or L'Ermitage. Jed Prouty's is the town's established eating and drinking spot, and its dark shutters, white clapboard siding, and full-length front porch proclaim it to have been a traditional inn. There is a carved granite watering fountain in front for horses that have long since deserted the town thoroughfares. Across the street from it is Rufus Googins Park and its river walk.

The most creative cuisine can be found at L'Ermitage, a supper favorite for couples, which has limited seating. MacLeod's is the most popular restaurant, combining Yankee cooking and modern touches in a manner that pleases a variety of palates. The restaurant's walls are hung with large black and white photographs of nineteenth-century maritime Bucksport at work, which provides a nice feeling of local history.

For a deeper feel for local history, there is the Bucksport Historical Society Museum, on Main Street between the local Key Bank branch, which has the town's only automatic teller machine, and the Dockside Restaurant. Stoutly built of wood and painted white, the museum is a former Maine Central Railroad station left over from the days of passenger train service in Maine. It is open during July and August on Wednesdays, Thursdays, and Fridays between 1:00 and 4:00 P.M., and by appointment.

Among the memorabilia on display in the museum are photographs of the local Farnum brothers, who found fame and fortune in the theatrical world. William Farnum starred in the early movie version of *Ben Hur*; Dustin Farnum starred in *The Virginian*. There are photographs of film star Joel McCrae visiting relatives and friends in Bucksport in the 1940s and 1950s. Suspended near the ceiling is one of the whaleboats that was mass-produced here around the turn of the century. The whaleboats were crafted at the corner of Mill and Main Streets inside a building that now houses a sandwich shop.

Next door to the former whaleboat building shop is the cemetery where the town's founder, Jonathan Buck, is buried beneath a granite monolith that also seems to be one of the town's major tourist attractions. After a rainstorm or on a drizzly day, knots of people stand outside the cemetery, peering and pointing through the wrought-iron fence at Buck's tombstone. They are looking at a fault in the granite that is highlighted by water and that is said to be the outline of the leg of a woman who was sorely wronged by Buck and cursed him. The cemetery is uphill from the site of Buck's original home and sawmill, which were burned by the British during the Revolution. All are opposite the town's only shopping center, which contains a supermarket whose deli counter offers ready-made and made-to-order sandwiches.

If you want a sense of how maritime Bucksport looked, take a drive among the handsome homes on Franklin Street. It parallels Main Street and is just above it on the slope of land where most of the town's residences nestle. Also drive down MacDonald Street or one of the other streets between Franklin and Main that run down to the river.

Stroll the town's river walk, where ship construction once flourished at the yards along the now-grass-covered shore. The remains of marine railways and stagings are still visible at low tide. The first recorded vessel launched here was the sixty-ton *Hannah,* built during 1770–71 when the town was known as Buckstown. Hundreds of vessels followed, including several privateers built between the Revolution and the War of 1812.

Near the Champion mill end of Franklin Street, on the uphill side of the road, is a partially concealed, ramshackle complex that began life in 1848 as the Methodist Church's Eastern Maine Conference Seminary, which can be seen from Fort Knox. The Roman Catholic Church bought the complex in 1940, changing it to St. Joseph Oblate Seminary. It was closed in the 1970s, after which part of the complex was used for public housing.

Just east of Bucksport is H.O.M.E., a sprawling complex of retail shops and work spaces beside US 1/State 3. Founded more than twenty years ago as a private spinoff of President Lyndon B. Johnson's war on poverty, H.O.M.E. (which stands for Homeworkers Organized for More Employment) thrives on donations as well as sales of local crafts, especially woven articles, pottery, and wooden toys and accessories.

Bucksport is best viewed from a distance, and the best place to view it is across the river in Prospect, from Fort Knox's granite parapets, gun ports, rifle galleries, and grass-covered earthworks. Fort Knox nestles into the side of a wooded bluff that rises above the Penobscot. Its upper works provide not only a marvelous view of Bucksport but of the Penobscot River as it rolls seaward.

Construction of Fort Knox, which was never completed, was begun in the 1830s during a now generally forgotten episode in North American history known as the Aroostook War. It was an eastern range war in which timber, not cattle, were the issue, and the combatants were timber barons and lumberjacks rather than cattle barons and cowboys. During one of the warmer moments of the dispute, the government in Washington ordered Fort Knox built as a deterrent to the British taking over the Penobscot area, as the redcoats had done during the Revolution and the War of 1812. The fort was to be part of an extensive coastal defense system. The granite for it was cut at nearby Mount Waldo in Frankfort and, after being barged downriver, was fitted together on the bluff opposite Bucksport. Stone needed for the forts being built in Portland Harbor was also cut and shipped from the Penobscot Bay area.

The shore defenses were never tested, even during the Civil War, when Adm. Raphael Semmes, captain of the Confederate sea raider *Alabama* ventured into the Gulf of Maine to terrorize Yankee shipping. But the still-incomplete Fort Knox was used to train Maine regiments, including the 20th, which gained fame at Gettysburg. And during the Spanish-American War, the fort was garrisoned by Connecticut National Guardsmen. But there has never been an angry shot fired at or from Fort Knox.

If you are approaching Bucksport from the west side of Penobscot Bay, take the left immediately before the Waldo-Hancock Bridge onto State 174 and you will be at Fort Knox (nominal fee). Bring a flashlight to better explore the maze of passageways.

Fort Knox and the Waldo-Hancock Bridge across the Penobscot River as seen from Bucksport

Just before the bridge on the right are two scenic turnouts positioned along the Penobscot Narrows. They offer good views of the Narrows with Bucksport at one end and Penobscot Bay at the other. The brownish color of the river comes from the watershed's hundreds of square miles of forest and bog.

The land mass to the east across the river is Verona Island, which is formed by the river forking at Bucksport. Earlier in this century, saltwater farm–based river pilots on Verona Island would halt what they were doing at the sight or sound of a vessel and, as their forebears had done, row out to the approaching ship to clamber aboard off Fort Point to guide the ship upriver.

Between the bridge and the second turnout is the Sail-Inn Restaurant, a former tavern that now has scenery on tap along with breakfast or lunch under umbrella-shaded tables during good weather. There is also an inside dining room. The Sail-Inn is worth a stop to gaze at the upper bay, which when the sun slants across it can dance with a magical metallic shimmer.

When you cross the Waldo-Hancock Bridge over the Penobscot Narrows onto Verona Island, you'll see an osprey nest atop the east tower—the indication that you're about to enter Down East. To see the site of Bucksport's most significant maritime event, turn left to the Verona Island boat launching ramp just before the second and final bridge to Bucksport. From this site on March 23, 1905, was launched the Arctic exploration vessel *Roosevelt,* which Adm. Robert E. Peary used as a base for his successful dog-sled dash to the North Pole..

The *Roosevelt* remains the most celebrated vessel launched from an area yard. You can see where the steel-sheathed hull gathered momentum on its way to the water.

The *Roosevelt's* design, largely by Peary, had been inspired in part by another polar exploration vessel, *Fram*, in which Norwegian explorer Fridjof Nansen drifted in ice through North America's Northwest Passage.

The hulls of both vessels were configured so they would rise when grasped by ice rather than be crushed. The money for the *Roosevelt* had been guaranteed at a meeting in a Bar Harbor cottage owned by Morris Jesup, Peary's major financial backer and president of the Peary Arctic Club. The ruggedly built, sail-assisted, steam-powered *Roosevelt* would do what it had been designed to do, buck through Arctic ice floes to put Peary in position for his sled-dog dash to the Pole and then be able to remain on station. On July 16, 1905, during an oppressive heat wave, the vessel sailed from New York where it had been outfitted and after farewell stops at Bar Harbor and North Sydney, Nova Scotia, headed for the land of the Inuit.

The first vessel built in the United States specifically for polar exploration, the *Roosevelt* was christened with a bottle of champagne encased in a block of ice by Mrs. Peary, who shattered both against *Roosevelt's* hull as the vessel slid stern first down the ways of the McKay and Dix Shipyard into the Penobscot. Hundreds cheered as the 184-foot vessel floated free. The launch site is now covered with a strip of asphalt, but there are still visible traces of the McKay and Dix yard and the Beazely Shipyard, which preceded it. The site is one of the best places to survey the Bucksport waterfront and to watch the annual round-Verona Island kayak and canoe race in autumn. Verona also has a small public park, a campground, and at least two sandwich shops, all staggered along a short strip of US 1/State 3.

You can get to Bangor from the south on either side of the river, but the most scenic side is the west side (the same side as Fort Knox).

Turn right when you exit the Fort Knox parking lot and stay on State 174 (to the right is a fine view of Mount Waldo) until it joins US 1A in Prospect. There is also a good view of the South Branch of Marsh Stream and its salt marsh as the road descends to it.

In Prospect, US 1A runs beside working and abandoned farms, and then beside the South and North Branches of the Marsh River as they commingle at the base of Mount Waldo. The town of Frankfort has created a park here around a state boat launching ramp, and from it through a gap in the hills bordering the Penobscot River is a view of the Penobscot at its widest, the Frankfort Flats. The park rests on the remains of granite company wharves where sailing vessels bound for major U.S. ports once took on cargoes of stone. Blocks of cut granite can still be seen strewn about in the marsh grass and high up on Mount Waldo. Frankfort once had a sizable trading fleet, and in the 1850s seven clippers were built along its shores.

The top of Mount Waldo is a good place from which to survey the area, and the fall foliage season is the best time to do it. It takes about thirty minutes to get to the quarry by walking straight up the old quarry track, a continuation of the Old Wharf Road (or Mount Waldo Road) in Frankfort. Before hiking up the mountain, it is a good idea to check at the Frankfort Town Office for maps of the area and parking advice.

The Old Wharf Road leaves US 1A almost directly opposite the town park. You can drive up this well-maintained gravel and dirt track, which runs back through the woods for several thousand yards beside Mount Waldo Brook, passing beneath a rusting railway trestle before intersecting with the paved surface of the Old Belfast Road, which is not marked. Turn right onto the Old Belfast Road, and almost as soon as you straighten your wheels, turn left back onto the Old Wharf Road. This was the route over which huge slabs of granite were brought down from the mountain by a primitive railway system.

No road signs mark the final turn onto the Old Wharf Road (or the Mount Waldo Road if you like), but a profusion of signs reading "No Parking" and "No Unauthorized Vehicles" identify it. About a hundred yards along the forest-bordered road, it erodes into a track and begins a sharp ascent just beyond a metal gate. Signs and a barricade are there to discourage area youths from driving to the partially flooded quarry. The tall wooden masts of the nineteenth-century derricks, held erect by guy wires anchored in granite, still rise high above the quarry. A rope dangles from one of the wires for swimmers to swing themselves into the water.

Mount Waldo's bird's-eye view of Marsh Bay and the Frankfort Flats surrounded by a softly undulating carpet of forest is superb. With determination, wilderness navigation skills, and careful stepping, because of loose rocks, you can reach the summit and its 360-degree visual sweep of Penobscot Bay, the Camden Hills, Bangor, the Dedham hills, and Blue Hill.

There is an easier way to the summit, which skips the quarry altogether, but it requires threading along hogbacked, gravel and dirt tracks in Prospect. As a start in asking directions, try the Prospect Volunteer Fire Department and Community Building, at the intersection of State 174 and US 1A. If it is closed, which is not unusual, try the general store opposite it. There is nothing mysterious about the easier approach to the summit other than it is easy to get lost finding it and it is easy to get lost climbing the mountain.

The next community beyond Frankfort is Winterport (it once was the winter port for Bangor), which has pleasing homes and buildings and interesting side streets running down to the river. There is a marina here for pleasure boats.

Thousands of tons of eggs, bound for Arab countries to be used as a source of protein, have been shipped through Winterport from all over the eastern United States and Canada. Tons of frozen chicken parts are shipped from here to Haiti. In what many people thought was going to be a sustained moment of economic revival in the 1970s, millions of tons of Aroostook County potatoes were shipped from Winterport to Europe to offset a bad potato harvest. The bonanza bubble burst before it was fully inflated, but the shipping flurry renewed interest in Maine in revitalizing its maritime links with the world.

Beyond Winterport is Hampden, a bedroom community of Bangor and the birthplace on April 4, 1802, of Dorothea Lynde Dix. Before she died in 1887, Miss Dix brought about sweeping reforms in the treatment of the insane in the United States, as well as reforms in prisons, jails, and poorhouses.

Early in this century Hampden set aside a park in her memory for rest and recreation. Fixed barbecues are positioned beside randomly placed picnic tables under a well-trimmed copse of trees. Green grass abounds. There is even a swing, and a trail that winds down a wooded slope toward the river.

A more well known person with a Hampden connection is horror writer Stephen King, who once taught English at Hampden Academy, near the center of town.

The Turtle Head Marina is at the end of a short side road and nestled by one of the most attractive sections of the river, near the site of a nineteenth-century boating club. There is a snack bar (in season), picnic tables, and room to walk about and look at boats and the ebb and flow of the tide. The site is just above Crosby Narrows, the closest thing to a chasm on this section of the river. Several thousand yards upriver is the Snow and Neally Company, a family business that began making axes and peaveys (they were invented in Bangor) when timber was king. The business continues today selling axes and splitting mauls through L.L. Bean in Freeport and other outlets. Just beyond is a local landmark, the Tin Bridge, which marks the beginning of the city of Bangor.

In the nineteenth century, Bangor was a major international lumber port. Its sawmills operated round the clock to meet world demand. The mills of the Queen City of the North, as Bangor dubbed itself, were a marvel of their day, so much so that New England's leading literary intellectual, Ralph Waldo Emerson, came to witness what many thought was the industrial age gone mad.

But Bangor's time in the sun was brief. The wood and stone cribwork used to support ice chutes and to boom timber waiting to be loaded aboard ships can still be seen in the river.

With the dual collapses of the Maine timber industry and the state's wooden shipbuilding industry in the 1880s, the economic plug was pulled on the city. It has not yet recovered its former vitality, but its citizenry has a penchant for setting recoveries in motion. If you like being a historical detective, this is what makes it a city worth seeing. River excursion boats have been operating on an irregular basis from the municipal marina in Bangor for the past several years. If you want to make certain about a boat, call the Chamber of Commerce.

Bangor is the financial and wholesale and retail distribution center for northern and eastern Maine. Air more than water is now Bangor's link to trade, and its airport, Bangor International, offers trans-Atlantic flight service and air freight shipments.

The nineteenth-century timber boom encouraged Bangorians to make great plans for their city, which was laid out with sweeping parks surrounded by fine residential districts, and a commercial and financial district set off by public gardens. Much of what was begun remains—the parks; fine residential areas; a still-splendid library that was once one of the best in the nation; the Bangor Symphony Orchestra, the nation's oldest municipal symphony; and some fine architectural designs that are scattered about the city like so many mislaid gems. The Chamber of Commerce, whose office is in Bass Park, sponsors bus tours of Bangor's architectural past.

There is a definite sense of city in Bangor, despite its population of less than 40,000. One of its subtle atmosphere enhancers is the twelve-acre campus of Bangor Theological Seminary, whose activity and blend of nineteenth- and twentieth-century buildings lies between Hammond and Union Streets at the edge of the old commercial district. The campus embraces a former residence of Hannibal Hamlin, President Lincoln's first vice president.

Although Bangor's old commercial district lost some of its best buildings during the urban renewal of the mid-1900s, the prosperity of the 1980s resulted in new vitality for the downtown area. Building fronts were painted in rediscovered historical colors. Parks were restored, and yuppy eateries, coffee shops, and bars began popping up in storefronts. The city began a serious and partially successful effort to revitalize its long-dormant waterfront and to attract a marine industry.

The Penobscot Plaza shopping complex along the river marks the site of Bangor's Union Station, where until the mid-1900s many summer residents bound for Mount Desert Island stepped off the train and onto the Penobscot River ferry *Bon Ton*. Once on the far shore, they boarded waiting motor vehicles. The Joshua Chamberlain Bridge, named for the commander of the 20th Maine Regiment, marks the *Bon Ton's* route.

Bangor's major rite of spring is the annual Kenduskeag Stream Race, which is observed by thousands and participated in by hundreds. It is an end-to-winter celebration, even if sometimes blue-lipped canoeists and kayakers maneuver the frigid, rushing waters of the Kenduskeag in driving snow.

Paul Bunyan, the legendary logger, has become associated with Michigan and the Pacific Northwest, but he originated here before moving west with the logging industry, and Bangor has preserved a statue of the giant lumberjack. Paul's head and shoulders are visible in the treetops of Bass Park, which fronts on Main Street beside the *Bangor Daily News*, Maine's largest daily newspaper. The city's fairgrounds/bandstand/harness racing track is located at Bass Park. Snowmobile racers converge on the track in winter, and in Bangor and adjacent communities there are organized cross-country ski races each year.

Farther along Main Street, toward the downtown, is Davenport Park, where the bow plate of the ill-fated battleship *Maine* is displayed. Diagonally across Main Street from the park is the brick structure of the former Bangor House, a national landmark that has accommodated presidents and prostitutes and now is a haven for the elderly and the disabled.

In the center of downtown Bangor is a work by Castine sculptor Clark Fitz-Gerald, whose work in metal is admired on both sides of the Atlantic. In the public garden beside Kenduskeag Stream is a statue of Hannibal Hamlin, who died in Bangor while playing cards downtown at a private club. In addition to being Lincoln's first vice president, Hamlin was one of his chief advisers during the Civil War and a governor of Maine.

Down Harlow Street in a tree-shaded park beside the city's Greek Revival library is the city's artistic diamond, a cast bronze representation of Bangor's once-famous river drivers, known as the Bangor Tigers, which was cast by Waldo Peirce. Peirce's art, particularly his paintings, earned him international acclaim early in this century. A native Mainer, he was a Lost Generation crony of novelist Ernest Hemingway.

North of Bangor is the city's main burial ground, Mount Hope Cemetery, which was inspired by Boston's Mount Auburn Cemetery. Off to one side, away from the marble monuments and lush landscaping, are the graves of unidentified river drivers, whose tombstones face the river in which they lost their lives driving logs to Bangor.

Drama on the river is now pretty much confined to the annual spring Atlantic salmon run. Fly fishermen, along with the occasional seal, try their luck from the North Brewer shore across the Penobscot. The first salmon caught by a human is sent to the United States president, a tradition that began with President William Howard Taft, a man of capacious intellect and appetite.

Brewer was a shipbuilding center and, like so many other Maine communities, an ice exporter. The remains of the shipyards are not easy to see, but the supports for ice chutes, which were used to slide ice from storehouses along the shore into the holds of waiting ships in the river, can still be seen. South Brewer is anchored by the pleasing lines of the turn-of-the-century Eastern Fine Paper Company, a model mill in its day and still an area mainstay that now makes recycled paper.

In North Brewer is the Maine Sardine Council building, located on the river side of North Main Street, where you can get complementary cans of sardines along with brochures about Maine's sardine industry.

State 15, known locally as the River Road, heads south through South Brewer to Orrington, which once had working farms and a fleet of twenty-five commercial vessels but is now another bedroom community of Bangor. Orrington was once connected to Hampden, across the river, by a ferry whose Orrington terminus was at the bottom of the Ferry Road, just below Crosby Narrows. Orrington's Sylvanus Snow wrote *The Maritime History of Maine*. Snow, who came from the area of Snow's Corner in Orrington, was one of a hundred American volunteers who served in the British Royal Navy with Lord Nelson on his flagship HMS *Victory* during the Battle of Trafalgar.

A few miles farther toward Bucksport and just beyond the Jet Diner is the entrance, on the right, to a riverside park maintained by the town of Orrington—not a bad place for picnicking.

From here it is only about twenty minutes back to Bucksport.

9
Castine, Stonington, and Blue Hill

Castine is one of the most charming and historically stormy villages in the state. It displays its history silently. Each spring Castine's three public works employees take a collection of hand-lettered signs out of winter storage and place them along the town's streets for summer viewing. In fall, they reverse the procedure. The handsomely decorated signs randomly unfold the community's history, providing glimpses into Castine's past as a seventeenth-century Massachusetts Bay Colony trading post, a seventeenth- and eighteenth-century French trading post of old Acadia, a United Empire Loyalist center during the American Revolution, and the proposed capital of New Ireland.

By the late 1700s, Castine rivaled Portland and Gloucester, Massachusetts, in maritime importance, and it was the salt port for an area stretching from Thomaston to Mount Desert Island. Revenues from these industries built the fine houses on Castine's elm-shaded Main Street. Salt was used as a preservative in commercial fishing, and it was used in massive amounts as a preservative in wooden ship construction. The salt was brought from Spain and Italy in Castine-built vessels, then packed along the keel, frames, and timbers of new ships to be absorbed by the vessels as they took form on the shore. In addition to the fourteen shipyards that once were strung along the crescent of Castine's waterfront, there were salt warehouses along Sea Street from which salt was dispensed to the 500 to 600 fishing vessels that visited annually. The Reef, a barroom, now occupies the cellar of a former salt warehouse.

Castine, Deer Isle, Stonington, and Blue Hill are the points of a triangular area protruding into Penobscot Bay that provide some of the best touring in the state. The historical signs in Castine, which can be seen by walking or driving, offer a crash course in Down East history—good reason to visit Castine first.

About two miles east of Bucksport on US 1/State 3 is the right-hand turn onto State 175, the Castine Road. In the distance on the left is the distinctive fir-fringed granite pate of Great Pond Mountain.

A slow, sinuous, downhill glide brings you to the center of Orland village, which for generations has operated one of the state's oldest municipal alewife harvests from the Narramissic River. The Orland Market is a good place to pick up a sandwich or a cup of coffee before the fifteen-mile journey to Castine.

The road curves and undulates, passing by the barely noticeable remains of a brick works, a never-completed railway roadbed once intended to link Castine to Bucksport, and a cluster of former quarrymen's and peat miners' houses in an area known as Hardscrabble. Where State 175 turns right toward Blue Hill, State 166 goes straight to Castine.

Castine used to be a full-fledged island at high tide, until British troops dug a ditch across the boggy neck that connects the village to the mainland and made Castine an island at low tide as well. The ditch is known as the British Canal.

Later, small bridges were placed at either end of the canal. The bridge on the harbor side, or Bagaduce River side, of Castine is now the only bridge, since the bridge on the Penobscot Bay side became a causeway. The bridge, which is little more than a culvert in the roadway, is the main entrance to town. Once over the canal, the road sweeps to the left up Windmill Hill, and at the top bends sharply to the right through a golf course that was once pasture. Battle Avenue continues along the spine of the island to Dice Head and the Castine lighthouse. All roads to the left lead down to the village one way or another.

On the right after the golf course and tennis courts is a Victorian-era farmhouse that is used by the Castine Golf Club, one of the nation's oldest. Almost opposite is the beginning of the Maine Maritime Academy campus. It, along with five other state-funded academies and the federally funded U.S. Merchant Marine Academy at Kings Point, New York, mints officers for the U.S. Merchant Marine. The academy is Castine's economic mainstay.

The campus is at the corner of Main Street, which descends to the waterfront and the commercial district. Here you'll find a number of good eateries, an art gallery, and several shops. Nearby is Eaton's Boat Yard, which still hauls and launches boats on its wooden railway with the aid of a donkey engine. Notices placed about town describe local sailboat charters. Most of the shops have free walking tour brochures, which unfold into street maps.

Maine Maritime Academy, founded here in 1941, occupies a large portion of the town, sprawling halfway down the hill in brick Victorian buildings of the former Castine Normal School (a teacher's college), former private residences, and modern buildings. On the waterfront are moored the massive academy training ship as well as the veteran Arctic exploration schooner *Bowdoin,* a classic wooden vessel designated a National Historic Landmark. The double-planked, eighty-four-foot *Bowdoin* was launched in 1921 from Hodgdon Brothers Shipyard in East Boothbay and made fifty-four trips to the Arctic under Adm. Donald B. MacMillan.

Amerindians first visited this area on a regular basis, then the Pilgrims established a fur trading post. They in turn were displaced by the French. In the contest between the English and the French for North America, Castine was captured and recaptured, and was briefly taken by the Dutch, who had also been vying for North America. The literal tug-of-war over Castine ended in 1756 when England finally defeated France.

The fledgling trading community was alarmed by the growing concentration of rebels in the Camden area who were interfering with the commerce of Castine and other East Penobscot Bay communities. One target of the rebels was sailing vessels carrying firewood to British garrisoned in Boston. A Castine deputation went to Halifax, Nova Scotia, then more than Boston the area's cultural and commercial center, to petition for protection. The Crown was not overjoyed by the request, but it agreed to send a garrison. What it sent was probably not what Castine had expected.

In the summer of 1779, three years into the American Revolution, British transports arrived at Castine to deposit 800 officers and men ashore. The men were mostly fifteen- and sixteen-year-old Scots who had never seen action. Fortunately for them their commander was General MacLean, a man in his fifties who had seen more campaigns than his troops had years. The other senior English officers with him were seasoned combat veterans. Bolstering the Scottish infantry was a unit of the Royal Irish Artillery. While they were establishing defensive perimeters and encouraging area people to sign loyalty oaths, the Royal Navy, represented by three small warships, kept the forty-vessel American fleet at bay. The arrival of British reinforcements routed the American fleet up the Penobscot River, where vessels not set afire by British gunners were run aground and often set afire or blown up by their American crews.

In short, the British acted adeptly and the Americans ineptly. The debacle was so embarrassing to the United States that, with a few exceptions, it is not mentioned even today in public school textbooks. It certainly casts Paul Revere, the ordnance officer, and Commodore Dudley Saltonstall, leader of what was called the Penobscot Expedition, into a very unsavory historical soup.

The American force, which had begun landing at points other than Dice Head, got lost in the dense undergrowth and began spilling out of the woods by the fort in confusion. The British commander, who had decided to surrender at the first show of respectable force by the rebels, stood by the fort's flagpole, his hand on the flag halyard, ready to strike the Union Jack at the first bit of force displayed by the Americans. Unfortunately for MacLean's plan, the attackers continued to mill about in confusion at the edge of the woods. And then the worst of all possible things happened. The British, in putting up what was to be a respectable resistance before surrendering, drove the Americans back into the woods. MacLean took his hand from the flag halyard and prepared for the siege of Castine. Both sides settled into routines, each awaiting reinforcements. During the wait the British made much progress on Fort George, but the fort was not solid enough to contain the American prisoner, Gen. Peleg Wadsworth, who escaped under cover of a dark and stormy night, at one point wading across the cove that now bears his name. His poet grandson would make one of the expedition's leaders famous with his poem "Paul Revere's Ride."

Back at Castine the British garrison continued to hire local residents to complete Fort George, which was becoming the centerpiece of a network of fortifications. Harassed, battered, and fearful Loyalists from New England, New York, New Jersey, and Pennsylvania began to seek refuge at Castine. At the time it was thought that if the rebellious thirteen colonies actually became independent, their northeastern border would be the center line of Penobscot Bay. To protect Nova Scotia from the social foment of the new nation, a buffer colony to be called New Ireland would be established between the Penobscot and the St. Croix River estuary. The new province would be a cushion between New England and Nova Scotia (New Scotland). Its capital would be Castine, the burgeoning United Empire Loyalist center.

Unfortunately for New Ireland, the St. Croix, not the Penobscot, was chosen as the boundary when the Revolution ended, and the buffer colony was named New Brunswick in honor of King George III's House of Brunswick. The newly designed city of St. John would be its capital. The British garrison in Castine announced that anyone who wanted to be transported to the new fishing village of St. Andrews, New Brunswick, near St. John, could do so at Crown expense. About fifteen Castine homes were dismantled and placed on barges for the trip to St. Andrews, where they were taken ashore and reassembled. Several of them still stand today.

The British left Castine for the last time in 1815. The prosperity they had helped begin continued until the Civil War, but by the 1870s the town was going broke. Whether or not to encourage summer residency was the issue at a special town meeting in the early 1880s. Shortly after the vote, an article describing Castine as a new watering spa superior to overcrowded Bar Harbor appeared in *Century* magazine. The article was written by Noah Brooks, a nationally known newspaperman, author, one-time confidant of President Abraham Lincoln, and a Castine native. Retiring to his native town, Brooks set about writing novels for boys that describe life as it was when Brooks was growing up here. He began life on the Castine Common, beside the 1790 Bullfinch belfry–adorned Town Meeting Hall, now occupied by the Unitarian Church.

On the other side of the common, in the early nineteenth century, stood the courthouse and county jail. Across Court Street opposite the common is the site of a tavern that once provided food and drink for people doing business in the court. By 1840, the shiretown had been moved to Ellsworth.

In Brooks's day, Castine was divided into the North End and South End, each a latticework of neighborhoods. The two halves of town were divided by Main Street, popularly known as Quality Avenue. It was inhabited by successful salt traders, shipwrights, and ships' masters. The sailing vessels were owned by shareholders who represented a cross section of the town. On Water Street were sailors' boardinghouses, the homes of the less successful fishermen, and until about 1840 a brothel.

After the Civil War, Castine's era of prosperity ended. Residents of the once-bustling, internationally oriented trading community were now taking in summer boarders, and several inns catering to rusticators were in operation. The ringing of caulking hammers on the shore had long been stilled. Instead of

The training vessel State of Maine graces Castine Harbor when she's not crossing the Atlantic with Maine Maritime Academy students

shipbuilding, sardine and lobster canneries were now the activity on the waterfront.

The Pentagoet Inn and the Castine Inn, almost opposite each other on Main Street, are survivors of the period of transition to summer residency. Because the Pentagoet tends to cater fairly exclusively to its guests, its dining room is not as open to the public as those of the other inns. You usually need a reservation at the Castine Inn as well, but if it is not too busy a night, you can make a reservation while having a drink at the bar (one of the coziest in the area) or on the piazza, which overlooks Main Street as well as the inn's formal garden.

The Manor on Battle Avenue, which has a longer season than its Main Street cousins, occupies a huge, shingle-style "cottage" and concentrates on elegantly served gourmet meals. The same owner operates the Holiday House on Perkins Street whose rooms all have harbor views. Dining arrangements here are minimal, and because the inn is near two churches, there is no bar.

There is only one exit from Castine, and that is to backtrack on the road that leads into it. Veer right where State 166A splits from State 166, then take State 199 right toward Penobscot. At one point the road runs beside Northern Bay, a favorite winter hangout for Canada geese. At the head of the bay is a seasonal food take-out (good ice-cream cones) with picnic tables that overlook the water. Just past the church, which has a nearly year-round public supper on Saturday nights, is a turnout to the right with a picnic table beside the bay.

Northern Bay is a bulge in the Bagaduce River, which farther along its course constricts to form the Bagaduce Falls. This reversing falls is in North Brooksville, beside the Bagaduce Lunch, on State 176. The Bagaduce Lunch is a very good, homey, seasonal take-out in a roadside copse of evergreens. The owners have placed picnic tables on a sloping glade overlooking the falls.

Turn right at the T in the village of North Brooksville, a short distance from the Bagaduce Lunch and the bridge over Bagaduce Falls, and, using State 176 as a base line, explore the side roads running off to the right. One of them goes to Cape Rosier, on the north shore of which is the state-managed Holbrook Island Sanctuary. It offers trails, picnicking, and superb views of Penobscot Bay.

The coves along the cape's ragged southeasterly edge present a series of beautiful vistas and restful settings. Horseshoe Cove is a favorite way point for experienced sea kayakers who circumnavigate the cape by leaving Castine with Harborside to port and returning by paddling up Horseshoe Cove to a portage into Smith Cove and back to Castine.

Leaving the cape and returning to State 176 leads you to the village of South Brooksville and Buck's Harbor, which has a very respectable looking yacht club, a restaurant, and a cordial general store. The harbor is actually known to sailors as Buck Harbor, to distinguish it from the other Bucks Harbor that is farther Down East in Washington County.

State 176 joins State 175/State 15 south toward Deer Isle and past Caterpillar Hill, which provides a striking panorama of Penobscot Bay and its islands. There is a scenic turnout, a roadside picnic table, and a pleasant seasonal gift and sandwich shop. The landlocked body of water down the long, sloping blueberry barren is Walker Pond, a nineteenth-century center of winter ice harvesting activity. Partially visible in the middle distance is Eggemoggin Reach and the suspension bridge from the Sedgwick mainland to Little Deer Isle. When strong winds are hurtling down Eggemoggin Reach—that long corridor of water between the mainland and Little Deer Isle and Deer Isle—a drive over the suspension bridge can be exciting, but far less so now that the state has placed aerodynamic wind deflectors on the bridge's sides. They reduce buffeting, but they also block glimpses of the sparkling blue reach. During severe storms, spray flies across the causeway between Little Deer Isle and Deer Isle, sometimes making it impassable.

A side trip down Eggemoggin Road on Little Deer Isle ends at a public boat launching ramp and views of the east entrance to the reach, East Penobscot Bay, and the former Pumpkin Island Light station (now private), as well as the Brooksville shore and Buck's Harbor. On the southwest side of the island is Blastow Cove and Eaton's Lobster Pool, a popular dining spot known for its view and the food. The view from the causeway is splendid, and it makes it more splendid to know that before the causeway was built Deer Islers and Little Deer Islers raced full-rigged models of America's Cup competitors in the gut that once separated the two islands. The model racers knew current and tide well and timed their races so their hand-carved boats would come to rest on the shore with a falling tide and not be carried out to sea.

There are also good views of the reach on Deer Isle, along the Ferry Road (so named because a ferry once ran from it to the Sedgwick shore on the mainland) and also along the Reach Road (named because it runs beside the reach). Both leave State 15 to the left after the causeway.

British settlement of Deer Isle began around 1755, and by 1775 there were about a hundred families in the area making livings from seafaring, fishing, and farming. Shipping was a major contributor to the island's economy throughout the nineteenth century, and during the first half of it shipbuilding was the prime industry. By the late 1800s, there was a new endeavor on the island, granite. The heart of the industry was in Stonington, which became so much of a boomtown that in 1897 it separated from the town of Deer Isle.

Deer Isle village, displaced long ago by Stonington as the island's commercial center, is the softer, gentler community. In the village is a large, well-maintained, barn-shaped red structure once known as The Ark and more recently known as the Pilgrim's Inn.

It was inside The Ark in the last century that Deer Isle mariners were recruited for America's Cup crews. Deer Islers made up the entire crews of the America's Cup yachts *Defender* in 1895 and *Columbia* in 1899. Those were the days when yachtsmen hired professional crews, and Deer Isle, a repository of merchant mariners and commercial fishermen, had an abundance of skilled sailors. In the late 1800s, when Maine's maritime economy was in downturn, nearly a thousand Deer Islers were employed by the yachting industry. A visit to the Deer Isle Historical Society Museum and the Salome Sellers House, which occupy the same tract of land in Sunset, provides a quick insight into island culture. If the museum is closed, inquire locally about getting an appointment.

Sunset is a tiny village on the west side of the island, hence its name. On the opposite side of the island you might expect to find Sunrise; instead it is Sunshine. Located at the eastern end of Eggemoggin Reach, Sunshine has striking views of Mount Desert Island across the sweep of Blue Hill Bay. It is also home to the Haystack Mountain School of Crafts, a summer mecca for serious artists. Its presence helps explain the many art galleries scattered about the island.

All the through roads on Deer Isle eventually lead to Stonington, a maritime masterpiece that has been pocked by granite dust. Stonington has a major boatyard—known locally as The Shipyard—at one end, a lobster fishermen's cooperative at the other end, and a commercial fishing pier in the middle. The gaps are filled by a variety of commercial enterprises and residences, with the whole straggly line of mostly nineteenth-century buildings facing or backing up to Deer Island Thorofare, a watery lane formed by Deer Isle and a cluster of offshore islands. Among them is Isle au Haut, part of Acadia National Park. A mail/passenger boat to Isle au Haut leaves regularly from Stonington.

If there is one town on the Maine coast that looks the way people imagine a Maine fishing community to look, it is almost certainly Stonington. White clapboard houses, some with flowers growing beside them, nestle on a hillside pierced by granite outcroppings. The loudest sound is usually the raucous cry of seagulls swirling above the harbor and the whine of engines as fishing boats leave and return to their moorings.

At the west end of town, *Bill of Rights, Mayflower II,* and other American Sail Training Association–designated Tall Ships are brought to be repaired by local artisans. The Shipyard, which is Billings Diesel & Marine Service, is a major employer in

Hancock County. During World War II, it and other yards along the coast produced small craft for the U.S. Navy.

Stonington hosts lobster boat races in July and a Fishermen's Day in August. Both are excellent events and both turn the usually all-business commercial fish pier that extends into the harbor into a public promenade. Connie's and the Fishermen's Friend are the most popular restaurants in town.

Back on the mainland, State 175 east between Sargentville and Sedgwick along Eggemoggin Reach provides vistas of wildflowers, water, sky, and the low, fir tree–studded shore of Deer Isle. The Benjamin River at Sedgwick is a favorite anchorage for Penobscot Bay passenger schooners and, occasionally, the New York Yacht Club, as well as the home of the Benjamin River Boat Yard, and Arno Day, one of the area's premium boatbuilders.

As State 175 begins to emerge from the woods of West Brooklin, it runs by Bridges Point Boat Yard, which turns out the highly able and agile sloop the Bridges Point 24, as well commercial fishing vessels. Just beyond is Duffy & Duffy, whose motor yachts and fishing boats are sold throughout the Western Hemisphere and in Japan. The Brooklin Boat Yard, which has retained its specialization in classically designed wooden boats while adding an eclectic array of high-tech construction techniques to its repertoire, is down a side road just before Brooklin village. The yard also produces handsome rowing shells called Bangor Packets.

In Brooklin village is an excellent, small eatery, the Morning Moon Cafe. It is often full, particularly in summer, and people actually queue up outside. The convenience store across the intersection sells made-up sandwiches, which are fine for a picnic at Naskeag Point.

The road to Naskeag runs between the convenience store and the Morning Moon Cafe. *WoodenBoat* magazine, a gem of a publication, is on the way to Naskeag Point and is located on the rambling grounds of a former summer estate. It is worth a telephone call (there is a phone by the convenience store) to ask about touring the magazine's boatbuilding school.

In August one of the most beautiful maritime spectacles in the Northeast occurs here when an average of a hundred classic sailboats compete in the annual Eggemoggin Reach Regatta. The race begins and ends off the WoodenBoat School grounds, which are closed during the regatta to all except participants; but Naskeag Point and Sunshine on Deer Isle can be good vantage points. In September the Maine passenger schooner fleet holds a sail-in off Naskeag that is a marvelous sight.

Just offshore from the boat launching ramp at Naskeag Point is Harbor Island, where winter storm seas have exposed a large shell midden (mostly clamshells) left by Amerindians.

On the northeast side of Naskeag Point is Flye Point, and at its tip is The Lookout, which has an outstanding view and a well-run kitchen. There are two boatyards on the Flye Point Road, DPS Marine and Flye Point Marine. The former is a full-service yard with links to James Steele, who lives nearby and who builds one of the finest peapods on the Maine coast. The latter builds sturdy, highly maneuverable workboats for commercial fishermen. Flye Point and Naskeag Point are good areas to explore, but a four-wheel-drive vehicle is needed on the side roads.

There are some lovely views, both landward and seaward, along State 175 as it sweeps the length of Blue Hill Neck, where E. B. White once lived and wrote beside Blue Hill Bay. One of the area's most delightful views is at Carter Point, at the end of the neck, where water flows in and out of the Salt Pond with the tide. The immediate area is known as Blue Hill Falls, and the massive force of the water flow is a favorite with kayakers.

The best view of the Blue Hill area is from the top of Blue Hill itself. The crest has plenty of comfortable places to lie or sit, and almost every one of them presents a panorama of woods and water—lots of water.

The best way to get up the mountain is from the Mountain Road, which runs between State 15 and State 172 north approximately opposite the entrance to the Blue Hill Fairgrounds. There is an unofficial scenic turnout on the Mountain Road, just west of the Mountain Inn Bed and Breakfast, and opposite it is an unmarked but worn trail to the peak.

Back in the village, a golf course sprawls near Parker Point, and the town park, a pleasant place to picnic, is just beyond Blue Hill Memorial Hospital and the public boat landing, where lumber schooners once took on cargo. On the opposite side of the upper harbor is the site of the old steamship wharf, another good picnicking ground.

Blue Hill's two most enduringly popular restaurants, Jonathan's and the Firepond, are in the middle of the village, along with a summer cafe that overlooks the harbor, Jean-Paul Bistro. On the way to the town park are the Red Bag Deli, and a breakfast and lunch place, The Pantry, located at one end of a nineteenth-century brick commercial building. On State 172 on the way out of town is Sarah's, a breakfast, lunch, and dinner restaurant that also dispenses good ice-cream cones. Farther along State 172, almost to the fairgrounds, is the Left Bank Cafe (excellent pastry and live music), which is something of a New York delicatessen gone rural. One of the town's most popular restaurants is Pie in the Sky Pizza, which is tucked away on a side street behind the old commercial district. It serves fare as good as it is attractive and eclectic.

One of the area's biggest attractions is the summer concert series at Kneisel Hall. In winter the Congregational Church sponsors a series of concerts.

Pie in the Sky is a name appropriate for Blue Hill. In the late 1870s there were 600 people here digging for gold and silver and whatever else they thought they might find. The frenzied activity coincided with the collapse of Maine's shipping and shipbuilding industries. It was a last gasp of a dying economy done with flare. By 1880, speculators had floated mining stock valued at $25,000,000, and a mining exchange and a hotel named the Gold and Copper Exchange had opened in the village. The ore rush was over in 1883 (the first summer resident, a Bangor woman, arrived the year before) and by 1900 the town's population had dropped from 2,213 to 1,808. The void was being filled by summer residents and tourists. The Blue Hill Mineral Spring operated for a while and then failed.

The silver and gold fever that struck Blue Hill was started locally by a Col. William Darling, who is said to have gone insane after the gold fever subsided. He had a small copper mine, and when a man named William Stewart, who is credited by some with discovering Nevada's Comstock Lode, came to town, Darling regaled him with stories about silver. Stewart in turn regaled the Boston and New York newspapers, which were read by developers who hastened to Blue Hill.

There was a precedent for taking things from the ground in Blue Hill. In addition to a copper mine it had six granite quarries, which between 1875 and 1905 were operating pretty much full bore. Blue Hill granite was used in the construction of the Brooklyn Bridge, the New York Stock Exchange, and the Pittsburgh Post Office.

Another of the town's major attractions is Rowantrees Pottery, which uses locally dug manganese in glazing their distinctive work.

10

The Ellsworth Area

The best things about Ellsworth proper are its public library, beside the Union River; the old business district; the brightly colored, hand-painted crest on the side of City Hall; the Birdsacre Sanctuary; and the Colonel Black Mansion.

The best things about the Ellsworth area are its beaches, the opportunity for moderately priced aerial tours from Bar Harbor/Hancock County Airport in Trenton, and discount shopping.

The Ellsworth area is large and includes one of the most popular attractions in coastal Hancock County. It is the 120-year-old Craig Brook National Fish Hatchery, located down a side road off US 1/State 3 about midway between Bucksport and Ellsworth. The hatchery's site—adjacent to Alamoosook Lake and near Craig and Toddy Ponds, all popular freshwater swimming and boating spots—has a lot to do with its large number of visitors. It is also on the way to Acadia National Park.

The hatchery is at the base of Great Pond Mountain, whose summit has magnificent, long-distance views of the mountains of Acadia and the interior, which on clear days includes Mount Katahdin. The unmarked trail to the summit takes off from the dirt road just beyond the fish hatchery.

The Craig Brook hatchery made its debut in 1871 when 72,300 salmon eggs, which had been incubated in the basement of an old mill on Craig's Pond Brook, were packed in moss and sent to state-run hatcheries in Maine, Massachusetts, and Connecticut. It was the implementation of a plan begun in 1864 to restore Atlantic salmon to New England's rivers. The restocking continues today.

In Maine the resurgence of salmon runs in the Saco, Sheepscot, Penobscot, Union, Narraguagus, Machias, East Machias, Dennys, and the St. Croix Rivers owes much to Craig Brook National Fish Hatchery and the early experimentation by Dr. Charles Atkins, who became an internationally celebrated fish scientist.

The hatchery park on Alamoosook Lake is a good place to swim and picnic. (Craig Brook's satellite, Green Lake National Fish Hatchery, on State 180 just north of Ellsworth, offers the same opportunities.)

Ellsworth, farther east on US 1/State 3, is the shiretown of Hancock County and a shopping mecca where Down Easters from as far away as New Brunswick converge in search of bargains along with budget-minded tourists and summer residents. Shoppers and the administration of county government keep Ellsworth's economic heart pumping. In the last century, Ellsworth was a manufacturing center as well as a major lumber port. It was the home of a standby of the North American farm and ranch, the Davis buckboard. Designed by Henry E. Davis of Ellsworth, the buckboard was made here by the thousands, and marketed throughout the continent.

Largely because of its location between Bangor and Mount Desert Island, the Ellsworth area profited from the economic boom of the 1980s, and it remains the fastest growing area in the state. L.L. Bean, London Fog, Corning/Revere, Bass Shoe, Dexter Shoe, and Wal-Mart all have outlets along High Street, which is also US 1/State 3.

An idyllic haven from the commercial aspect of High Street is the 100-acre Stanwood Homestead Museum and Birdsacre Sanctuary on Beckwith Hill, overlooking High Street at the beginning of the Bar Harbor Road (State 3). The year-round sanctuary is named in honor of Cordelia Stanwood, an Ellsworth native, pioneer ornithologist, educator, author, and photographer.

Another respite from High Street can be found in the old commercial district, at the intersection of Main, State, and Water

Streets by the Union River, where charm still resides. The area is still recognizable from Civil War–era photographs. Several hundred feet up State Street hill from the intersection is the Ellsworth Public Library, a Federal-style, former residence beside the river. A tiny public park nestles between the river, the library parking lot, and the end of the brick commercial block that backs up to the river. Inside the library's basement gallery, whose windows face the river, works by area artists are often on display.

The river was once Ellsworth's lifeblood. It provided the power to operate its mills and electric lights, and it was the avenue used by the city's 150-vessel fleet to sail to and from world ports. Ellsworth was once second only to Bangor as a lumber port. That may be difficult to believe, surveying the harbor from the Ellsworth Waterfront Park and Marina, because there is little visible evidence of past maritime activity. The park and marina are located in a section along Water Street that was once known as The Bowery, which got its name for the same reason as New York City's famous Bowery—named for the arbors and farms that used to be there. Unfortunately for Ellsworth's Water Street, there was a period during the last century when it had a local reputation for cheap bars almost as infamous as those of New York's Bowery.

Today Water Street is, for about a half mile, an extension of the old downtown commercial district, which then blurs into a pleasant and older residential district before becoming the rural Bayside Road. The Bayside Road, which merges with US 3 in Trenton, just before the bridge to Mount Desert Island, is popular with local motorists as a way of bypassing High Street traffic. Another plus for the Bayside Road, other than its undulating course along Union River Bay and some interesting perspectives of Mount Desert Island, is that it leads to the Oak Point Lobster Pound, which provides a lobster dinner with views of Blue Hill and Union River Bays and Mount Desert Island.

One of Ellsworth's most attractive points of interest is the Colonel Black Mansion, the 1862 Georgian home of John Black, a colonel in the Ellsworth militia. The red-brick, white-pillared house became known as Woodlawn and by the early part of this century had become a residence for the colonel's descendants, one of whom in 1928 bequeathed it to the city of Ellsworth. Woodlawn is located on State 172 (West Main Street, also called the Surry Road), just a short distance from the intersection of West Main and Court Street.

The road to Woodlawn is also known as the Surry Road because it leads to and from that small community, which embraces Newbury Neck, where there is a bathing beach facing Union River Bay. The Newbury Neck Road runs off the Surry Road just beyond Surry village, whose biggest commercial enterprise is an excellent nursery, Surry Gardens. Coming from Ellsworth the nursery is on the left and the Newbury Neck Road is only about a mile beyond.

The Ellsworth area's three best saltwater beaches are east of the city, in Lamoine (named for one of Champlain's officers) and Marlboro.

Lamoine has two beaches, both on the same road—State 184, which runs off US 1 just outside of Ellsworth on the way farther Down East. The turnoff is to the right about a mile beyond the junction of US 1 and State 3, just before two local eating spots—Jordan's and White Birches. Jordan's Snack Bar has been popular for two or three generations; White Birches is an entertainment complex with a golf course, motel, bar, and restaurant with a view.

The first Lamoine beach, in Lamoine State Park, is identifiable about a quarter mile before its entrance by the granite and iron–staked fence along the tree-lined road. The park was a coaling station for the U.S. Navy during the nineteenth and early twentieth centuries, before the federal government deeded it to the state. The park is a bargain; a small fee provides you access to swimming, a boat launching facility, picnic tables, and campsites. The second beach, named Lamoine Beach, is at the end of State

Ellworth's beautiful First Congregational Church

184, a short distance down the road from the state park. It has the better view of the two beaches and much more the atmosphere of a saltwater beach. Bathers at Lamoine Beach have an unimpeded view of the expanse of Frenchman Bay. There is a small parking area but no other amenities.

Marlboro Beach is a little trickier to find, because it is accessible only by secondary roads. Probably the simplest way to get to it is by turning east onto State 204 from State 184 and staying on it till it ends in a T intersection with what is sometimes known as the Seal Point Road. Turn right onto the secondary road, hug the shoreline, and when you reach an area that looks vaguely like a forgotten bit of filled land by the sea, you have reached Marlboro Beach. Actually fairly attractive, it faces Raccoon Cove, Frenchman Bay, and the Skillings River, and it is seldom crowded. Small-boat commercial fishermen use it to launch and land their boats.

Not too far from here Capt. John Smith, the seventeenth-century explorer/entrepreneur, anchored for a few days while assessing the fisheries potential of Frenchman Bay. Local divers, who came across a concentrated assortment of broken crockery and bottles from the colonial period, believe they may have found the actual anchorage site, which is several miles off Hancock Point in the direction of Bar Harbor.

Hancock Point, east of Marlboro Beach, lies at the end of a piece of land known as Crabtree Neck, which protrudes into Frenchman Bay and can be seen across the Skillings River from Marlboro.

Beginning in the late nineteenth century, summer visitors were brought to Hancock Point from Bangor aboard Maine Central Railroad trains and from Bar Harbor by the Hancock/Bar Harbor ferry. In those days, steamboats linked Bar Harbor to Rockland, Portland, Boston, New York, and Philadelphia.

For a brief moment in time in the early 1920s, Hancock Point sported seventy restaurants and fifty-five lodging houses—about the same number of like establishments in Bar Harbor today. All except the Crocker House Country Inn, which was built in 1883 as a business establishment, have disappeared.

A relaxing idyll at Crocker House is as good a reason as any to visit Hancock Point, where nature now conceals evidence of the area's wanton flirtation with honky-tonkism. Other good reasons to visit the point are the views of Sullivan Harbor from the east side of Crabtree Neck, and Sullivan Falls, a tidal falls between Sullivan Harbor and Taunton Bay.

The right-hand turn off US 1 to Hancock Point is in the center of Hancock village. It is marked by a sign a few hundred feet before the turn and at the turn by a granite monument, which is partially obscured by trees and shrubs. Just beyond the turnoff is the noted French restaurant Le Domaine. Nearby is the Pierre Monteux School for Conductors, which offers community concerts when it is in session in summer. Both are legacies of Hancock Point's cosmopolitan past.

11
Mount Desert Island

On a clear day atop Cadillac Mountain, you can look eastward across Frenchman Bay to Schoodic Point, where seas explode and beetle over ancient, Ice Age–scarred rocks. Below, clustered white by the sea in a rumpled forest mantle, are the communities of Bar Harbor, Seal Harbor, Northeast Harbor, Southwest Harbor, and Bass Harbor. Raising your eyes, you can see into forever. The view from Cadillac's summit, the highest promontory on the East Coast, is a most gloriously clear panorama. At 1,530 feet, it may be a midget in the world of mountains, but it is the highest natural viewing stand on the east coast of the New World until you get to Rio de Janeiro, Brazil. The view from Cadillac is something like flight, blue vastness.

On the lichen-mottled granite dome of Cadillac, for centuries a landmark for mariners, you are near the uppermost limit of North America's southeast coast, which runs from below Florida to Nova Scotia, where the continent's northeast coast begins.

You can sense, not see, the divide, and you can feel it in an often chilling breeze, even in summer, that baffles over the bare-rock top of Cadillac and below wafts over sea cliffs. Nova Scotia is east-northeast over the horizon, a long day trip away by sailboat. It is only five hours away by the oceangoing ferry *Bluenose,* which in summer makes daily round-trips between Bar Harbor and Yarmouth, Nova Scotia.

Almost due south, about 200 miles distant, is Georges Bank, where a floating community of fishing vessels lurches up and down as their crews hunt for groundfish and scallops. Beyond is the azure Gulf Stream, crisscrossed by heavily laden commercial vessels bound in and out of Maine, Nova Scotian, and New Brunswick ports. You can't see them. They are too far out. About 1,000 miles beyond is Bermuda.

Cadillac is a showpiece of Acadia National Park, the National Park Service's only park in New England. The park's beauty is as lulling as it is arresting, and for long periods on a summer day it is difficult to imagine a more tranquil place to be than its natural sanctuaries. Those moments make visiting the island almost mandatory. If you can stretch those moments into several days, which is easiest to do in spring and fall, consider yourself blessed. Privacy is fleeting in a popular paradise.

It is especially fleeting between July 4 and Labor Day. Hikers take to a network of nature trails. Bicyclists and horseback riders (you can rent both bicycles and horses on the island) negotiate a pattern of carriage trails laid out by the late John D. Rockefeller, Jr., whose seasonal residency here helped set a tone, real and imagined, for later summer rusticators. That tone still lingers in places like Northeast Harbor and Seal Harbor.

Traffic is the island's bane in summer. The steamships that ferried people to the island in the nineteenth century are gone, and now everyone but cruising yachtsmen arrives in some form of vehicle, looking for clean air, blue skies, and cool nights. They all take turns at hiking, biking, bird-watching, leaf peeping (in the fall), camping, horseback riding, shopping, and people peeping.

You could could spend weeks exploring Mount Desert Island, its mountains other than Cadillac, and its offshore islands. So a good idea is to collect a map of the island and a handful of brochures at the Tourist Information Center on Thompson Island, which acts as a large stepping-stone between the mainland and Mount Desert Island.

A must stop should be Acadia National Park's Visitors Center, where you can get detailed maps of the park, its network of trails and carriage roads, and its history, flora, and fauna. The

This cobblestone bridge spanning Jordan Stream in Acadia National Park is the first in a series of sixteen bridges linking the park's carriage roads

visitors center is located just inside the park's main entrance at Hull's Cove, which is several miles down State 3 from Thompson Island, on the outskirts of Bar Harbor.

Mount Desert Island is almost cut in half by Somes Sound, which results in two separate looped road patterns. The larger of the two loops, which is formed by State 3 and State 198 on the eastern side of the island, links Bar Harbor, Otter Creek, Seal Harbor, and Northeast Harbor. The eastern side of the island has almost all of the dramatic scenery, most of the park, and all of the major summer communities, which is why such fashionable restaurants as The Burning Bush can be found tucked away beside State 3 in Otter Creek, a modest working community nestled by the hidden opulence of Seal Harbor.

The other, smaller loop is formed by State 102 and State 102A. It loosely circles the west side, known as the quiet side, of the island, which includes the island's oldest settlement, Somesville, as well as the working communities of Southwest Harbor, Bass Harbor, and Bernard, and the summer retreat of Pretty Marsh. In the early nineteenth century when agriculture and small industries buttressed the island's economy, the wildly scenic but barren east side was known as the Backside, a place where painters of the Luminist School congregated in summer. Their paintings of nature in the raw, accentuated by towering skies suggestive of hope and God, appealed to Victorians who saw depictions of robust nature symbolic of the industrial robustness of youthful America. First in a trickle and then in a stream, the rusticators began visiting what was still the Backside. The two loops that evolved on either side of the divide, once known as the French Line, are linked at Somesville and at the fork in the road opposite Thompson Island.

The difference between the two sides of the island is at its extreme in Bar Harbor. It was here that the nation's politically and financially powerful congregated each summer. But the social changes wrought by World War II capped by the Great Bar Harbor Fire of 1947 put an end to Bar Harbor as a summer retreat for the chic and wealthy. They have scattered themselves about the island, with large proportions of them now reclustered in Northeast Harbor, Seal Harbor, and to a lesser degree in Pretty Marsh.

Today's Bar Harbor is more cosmeticized honky-tonk than chic. There are good restaurants—gourmet, exotic, and granola— and some good ice-cream shops, candy shops, clothing and sporting goods stores, and gift shops, all generally pricey. Two of the most popular pricey restaurants are George's, on Stephens Lane behind a bank on Main Street, and The Opera House, on Cottage

129

Street. In the same category is Hampton Court, on State 3 near the ferry terminal. All require reservations. Less expensive but so popular that sometimes only the patient can gain entry is Miguel's on Rodick Street. There's also Epi Sub & Pizza, a popular, moderately priced, eat-in or take-out sandwich shop on Cottage Street near Main Street.

Bar Harbor is overflowing with eating and lodging establishments, and much of the fun is cruising in search of good places to eat, drink, shop, and sleep. There is a surprising variety of accommodations, from posh to very modest.

If you want to see what makes Bar Harbor different from other resorts, head down to the waterfront. There's a municipal parking lot on the town pier. If you're walking, cut through the park on Main Street and head downhill toward saltwater and fresh breezes.

The end of the pier is reserved for the commercial fishing vessels, which are often tied up there. In the harbor a variety of commercial and pleasure boats toss at their moorings. The municipal ramps and floats on the east side of the pier are used by cruise ships to bring passengers and crew ashore for island excursions. About twenty-five world-ranging cruise ships, including *Queen Elizabeth 2,* have been dropping their hooks off Bar Harbor each summer as they cruise the New England and Canadian Maritime coasts. If you want to get a better look at one of the large vessels, take the paved public walkway that runs from the east side of the pier through the park toward the Bar Harbor Motor Inn (an elegant, rambling, Victorian-style structure with an ornate and excellent dining room). You can save the dining room for later and stay on the walkway (called the Shore Path). The Shore Path leads you between the sea and an array of summer homes. In about a mile, the path runs beside the dead ends of Albert Meadow and Wayman Lane, both of which lead to Main Street.

The excursion vessels tied up along Bar Harbor's waterfront provide trips into Frenchman Bay and the Gulf of Maine. The view of Mount Desert Island from the spray-flecked deck of a schooner under sail is one of the richest experiences you can give yourself. You can also take off on your own in a rental boat.

The three-masted, gaff-rigged excursion schooner *Natalie Todd* is moored on the east side of the pier by the park. Built in 1941 as a schooner-dragger for New England's Georges Banks and Newfoundland's Grand Banks, she was rebuilt in Thomaston in 1986 as a passenger schooner. The *Todd* carries about twenty-five passengers on two-hour sails among the islands of Frenchman Bay.

On the opposite side of the pier, the Frenchman Bay Boating Company, operated by the Colliers, an island family, offers nature and sight-seeing cruises in large-capacity motor vessels as well as the steel-hulled, Bermudan-rigged schooner *Bay Lady*. The company also offers deep-sea fishing excursions.

A short walk on West Street along the harbor brings you to the Golden Anchor Pier, next to the Golden Anchor motel, where the steel-hulled motor vessel *Acadian Whale Watcher* takes passengers out about twenty-five miles to Mount Desert Rock, an area where lobster fishermen haul their traps and minke and humpback whales spout and sport as they break the surface.

Farther along West Street toward State 3 is the stained-shingle exterior of the Bar Harbor Club, once private and exclusive and now for sale. Walk around back and take a look at what remains of the terraced garden that runs down to the sea.

What remains of the Bar Harbor Club, and the comely homes along West Street and the Shore Path, are Bar Harbor's past. Very much in the present is Jackson Laboratory for Genetic Research, where scientists make regular contributions to world medicine and technicians breed several thousand laboratory mice annually that are flown to research centers around the world. The Jackson lab, just outside of town, backed up against an edge of Acadia National Park, gives scheduled tours. Mount Desert Island Biological Laboratory, in nearby Salisbury Cove, studies marine life. And College of the Atlantic, on the edge of town, offers, among other things, a curriculum in human ecology.

You can leave Bar Harbor by State 3, which takes you through Otter Creek and Seal Harbor before beginning a scenic approach to Northeast Harbor. Or you can take State 233, which goes by Kebo Valley Country Club, just outside Bar Harbor, and the year-round headquarters of Acadia National Park, a short distance beyond the golf course.

If you are headed out of Bar Harbor on State 3, swing through the park along Ocean Drive. As it curves sharply right after Sand Beach, you are presented with one of the most marvelous seascapes on the coast. A cascade of boulders sweeps along the shore; in the distance the sea, made aquamarine by shoals and sun, flashes its teeth against the sheer face of Otter Cliffs, an idyllic spot for a picnic lunch.

Thunder Hole, a tourist favorite, is along this stretch of road. It is where the sea rushes into a lateral chasm of its own carving to crash inside a loosely fitted chamber of rock. From a distance, the deep rumblings sound like cannons booming; when the sea is roiled from an offshore storm or when the tide is running strong, the boomings are punctuated by water pluming skyward from the chamber.

Another park favorite is the Jordan Pond House, famous for its tea and popovers served on a lawn sweeping down to Jordan Pond. The restaurant, which also serves lunch and dinner, has lovely gardens.

If you are approaching Northeast Harbor on State 3 from Otter Creek, two must-sees are the azaleas at Asticou Gardens, and the extensive plantings at Thuya Gardens.

The best place to park in Northeast Harbor can be found by taking a left onto Harborside Road as you come into town, and swinging down to the waterfront. There is a large parking lot, and if you are lucky enough to find a space in summer, you will be just a short walk from the commercial district, as well as where you should be if you intend to visit the Cranberry Isles. The one-story, wooden gray building between the parking lot and the water contains the harbormaster's office. A Beal and Bunker Ferry Company ticket booth is at one end of the building and public toilets are at the other. There is also a bank of public telephones and a water fountain.

In summer, Northeast Harbor offers one of the best boat shows in the state. Finely fitted and luxuriously appointed yachts, power and sail, are tied up at slips that run out from the granite bulkhead in front of the harbormaster's office. A lawn with public benches stretches between the bulkhead and the parking lot. The sweep of elegant boats in the harbor is better than most major boat shows and there is no admission charge.

Northeast Harbor is what Bar Harbor once was—a fashionable resort. It is probably one of New England's last old-style resorts, something of an endangered species. Its main street is one of the most charming and quietly chic on the coast. The Colonel's Deli, Bakery and Restaurant, at one end of Main Street, is an enduringly popular place to eat in or take out. So is Redfields, Provisions, and Soup and Sandwich. If you are interested in marine supplies, F. T. Brown's Trustworthy Hardware is a gem.

You can leave town on the Manchester Road, which curves back and forth from the sea through a residential area of well-kempt summer homes before merging with Sargeant Drive (State 3), which swings beside Somes Sound. Sargeant Drive provides superb views of the sound, the only fiord on the East Coast, as it meanders along the base of Norumbega Mountain. The top of Norumbega and the summits of its sisters on the opposite shore, Acadia and St. Sauveur Mountains, offer the best views. Norumbega is the highest, at 852 feet. If you want to look, you have to climb.

Heading north on Sargeant Drive, you can catch a glimpse of Hall Quarry, carved out of the opposite shore near the head of the sound. The jumble of boats and buildings in front of the scarred rock is the John M. Williams Company, which builds comely boats from designs by Lyford Stanley of Bass Harbor, who is also one of the few remaining herring fishermen in the area. The large niches cut into the side of the sound's shoreline by nineteenth- and early twentieth-century quarrymen are now used by the Williams Company for winter boat storage.

At the head of the sound just before the junction of State 198 and State 233 is Abel's Lobster Pound, a tranquil dining spot in a tranquil setting that is complemented rather than marred by the bustling maritime operation below its pine-sheltered perch. The boat sheds at the bottom of the slope on which the restaurant is located are used for construction, repair, and restoration in sum- mer and boat storage in winter. You can combine dining with a look at yachts being made.

Sailboat racing is a major activity, and one of the best ways to watch it is to rent a boat for the day in Northeast or Southwest Harbor. Or find a vantage point at Seawall, south of Southwest Harbor; sometimes a leg of a race runs by there. You can find a vantage point in lower Somes Sound; or climb Flying Mountain, above Fernald Point in Southwest Harbor. Bring binoculars and a picnic lunch. If the race committee decides not to send the fleet your way, you can still enjoy the picnic and the view from Flying Mountain.

If scenic views are your objective and climbing is simply the means of achieving it, then, at 284 feet high, Flying Mountain should be your cup of tea. It is an easy climb through a copse of spruce, which is pleasant in itself, and the seaward view from the top is one of the best for the exertion on the island.

You get to the Flying Mountain trailhead by looping your way around the top of Somes Sound on State 198 to its junction with State 102 in Somesville. Turn left onto State 102 at the traf- fic light, and head for Southwest Harbor. As you make the down- hill approach to Southwest Harbor, you should see an IGA store on your left and shortly afterward signs for Fernald Point Road and the Causeway Club, also on the left. Turn onto the Fernald

Point Road and keep bearing left until you see signs for Acadia National Park and Flying Mountain.

In case you didn't notice when you passed through, Somesville is the oldest community on the island as well as the most charming. It is the quintessential setting for the twenty-odd white clapboard homes that are staggered along State 102 between the traffic lights at either end of the town. There is nothing here to attract tourists in numbers, which probably accounts for much of its charm—certainly its atmosphere of serenity. Somesville gets its name from Abraham Somes from Massachusetts, who located at the head of the sound in the eighteenth century and established mills by a stream. Today the stream and its millpond provide a haven for ducks.

Port in a Storm bookstore and A. V. Higgins Groceries are the only shops in the village proper. At the south end of town, where an amber caution light hangs over the roadway, is a road to the right leading to Beach Cliffs, a good picnic spot.

The amber light in Somesville also marks the summer location of Acadia Repertory Theatre. In the fall the theater troupe packs its makeup and wigs and heads back to Bangor, where it performs as the Penobscot Repertory Theatre throughout the winter.

Southwest Harbor is still recognizable in an 1850 painting by Luminist School painter Fitz Hugh Lane that depicts a lumber schooner taking on cargo from the Manset Shore. There is now a Coast Guard Group at Clark Point from which life-saving operations between Penobscot Bay and the Canadian border are orchestrated. The Clark Point Road is bordered on each side by pleasantly landscaped homes, commercial maritime enterprises, and the Claremont Hotel, a bastion of gentility where croquet is nurtured on a regulation pitch overlooking the entrance of Somes Sound. The Deckhouse beside the water is the nicest commercial spot on the island to have a late afternoon drink. Soft speech, sunsets, and fresh air are the order of the evening. Or enjoy the sunset at Beals Lobster Pound, beside the Coast Guard base at Clark Point. The working waterfront is concentrated along this section of the harbor, where fishing vessels churn to and from the sea, passing sleek sailing yachts built by the Henry R. Hinckley Company and Morris Yachts, Inc., two of North America's premium yacht builders. Tucked away behind two bungalows on the water side of Clark Point Road is one of the nation's finest crafters of wooden sailing and power vessels—Ralph W. Stanley, a legend in his own time. He has been featured in films and books and is a consultant for the U.S. Navy about the care and handling of the USS *Constitution* (Old Ironsides), which is on permanent display in Boston Harbor. Stanley, who is a member of one of the island's oldest families, is a popular lecturer at Maine historical societies as well as with wooden boatbuilders and boat buffs throughout New England. In his spare time he occasionally makes a violin.

You can get a look at some of Stanley's vessels from the Upper Town Dock off Clark Point Road. If a boat riding at its mooring has lovely, classic lines and is gaff rigged, it is probably Stanley built. If it is a wooden Friendship sloop, it has either been restored, repaired, or built by Stanley. It also may have been raced by him during one of the annual Friendship Sloop Society races at Boothbay Harbor. He is as skilled at sailing boats as he is at building them.

The Oceanarium, also near the Coast Guard base, provides a cornucopia of tidbits about the sea and the men and women who follow it. The volunteer guides are often retired and semi-retired fishermen.

The large sheds beside the Oceanarium and across the road from it are a combined operation of JBF Scientific, Inc., and its subsidiary, Southwest Boat Corporation. JBF designs and builds oil spill and debris recovery equipment vessels for use around the world. The U.S. Army Corps of Engineers has been a big buyer of JBF debris collectors, which it uses to help tidy the nation's waterways.

The T intersection of Clark Point Road and Main Street (State 102) is the center of Southwest Harbor's commercial district. One angle of the T is filled by McEachern & Hutchins hardware, which has a good marine supply section; an antique shop and art gallery are in the other angle. The six or seven restaurants running along and just off Main Street are all good. The Drydock Cafe and Inn and the Deacon's Seat are popular downtown eateries. Especially popular for breakfast is Randy and Gene's Kozy Kove, in the shopping mall beside Seal Cove Road: the baked goods are delicious and so is the coffee. Some of the late morning clientele who are in no hurry to leave are fishermen who have already put in a hard day's work, which they began before sunrise. Sawyer's Market, whose green-trimmed storefront on Main Street is something of a landmark, is one of the most charming stores on the island, as well as being an excellent grocery and source of picnic lunches.

In the parking lot behind Sawyer's is a very adequate, reasonably priced sandwich shop as well as the location of Aero-Hydro, Inc., whose founder, John Letcher, played a major role in winning the America's Cup back from the Australians in 1987. Letcher was the senior scientist for Dennis Connors's *Stars and Stripes* design team, which was headed by John Marshall, chief operating officer for The Hinckley Company in Manset. Interest in the America's Cup is fairly widespread on Mount Desert Island. Several island boatbuilders have supplied at least one tender to an American syndicate over the years or have personal or working associations with syndicate members. Building straightforward yachts, however, is the island's mainstay.

The Ship's Store in the Hinckley complex, which sprawls on the Manset shore on either side of the intersection of Mansell Lane and Alder Lane, has nautical supplies. Across the street is The Moorings, a popular eating and drinking establishment from which there are splendid views of the outer harbor and the entrance to Somes Sound.

A few hundred yards toward the inner harbor along Alder Lane is The Boathouse, which has an extensive marine supply and accessory shop as well as boat rentals, sail and power. At the head of the harbor are Mansell Boat Rentals and Great Harbor Marina (operated by Hinckley), both good places to rent boats. At the Manset Town Landing you can charter the topsail schooner *Rachel B. Jackson.*

South of town on State 102 is Seawall Restaurant, another eating and drinking establishment with a superb view from its dining room. The restaurant is at one end of a natural seawall that faces on Western Way and gives the area its name. Keep going for some of the most pleasant seascapes in Acadia National Park—Wonderland, Ship's Harbor, Bass Harbor Head Light, and the town of Bass Harbor. The lighthouse is a charming spot in a land of magnificent views, so park in the public lot and take a look.

Bass Harbor, until recent years, has been the island's last purely working harbor, and in a sense it still is. The predominant vessel in Bass Harbor is the lobster boat, and most of them are clustered off Thurston's Wharf on the Bernard side of the harbor. Most of the yachts you see tied up on the Bass Harbor and Bernard sides belong to Bass Harbor Marine, which is the Hinckley Company's charter division. The charter fleet is shuttled back and forth between Bass Harbor and the Caribbean.

The operations of Bass Harbor Marine and the Maine State Ferry Service almost physically merge at the water's edge, where the wash from the Swans Island ferry rocks charter fleet vessels at their moorings. If you are not in the mood to charter a yacht, you can always ride the Swans Island ferry. It is about forty minutes each way of blue sky and blue water bounded by fir-covered, granite-bordered islands. The same ferry also makes a run to Frenchboro on Long Island, which was once a rum-running repository during Prohibition. Large caches of whiskey, gin, and rum from Canada were off-loaded at Frenchboro for distribution to points along the coast by small craft. The harbor there has an enchanted qualty about it. Travel ashore is mostly by foot.

Unlike Frenchboro and most of the other offshore islands, Swans Island has an adequate road system. With a little enterprise you should be able to locate two of the nicest spots on the island, Fine Sand Beach and Hockamock Light.

Back in Bass Harbor, all of the places to eat are either near the ferry terminal or on the way from or to it. The place with the best view is probably The Deck House Restaurant and Cabaret Theatre, which is up the hill from the terminal and somewhat surrounded by Bass Harbor Marine operations. Another good view is from inside the dining room of the Seafood Ketch, which sits beside the harbor. With a window table and when the tide is in, you can dine within a few feet of the water and watch it form patterns in the sand. If you happen to be in the market for a sea kayak, turn onto McMullen Avenue and ask for Caribou Kayaks. It is run by Barry Buchanan, a precision-conscious craftsman who builds fast, sea-kindly kayaks.

The Bernard side of the harbor is clearly its residential side, where homeowners tend seaside gardens. Thurston's Wharf, conspicuous on the shoreline when looking across from Bass Harbor, is hardly noticeable as you drive along the Bernard shore, but look for it. Thurston's serves lobster and seafood from a deck overlooking the harbor. Before you get there, a road to the left will take you down to Bass Harbor Boat Corporation, where members of the Rich family have built boats since the eighteenth century.

If you turn left onto State 102 when you leave Bernard, you can take in the west side of the island all the way to Pretty Marsh and Town Hill. The scenery is less dramatic than the other side of the island, but there are more opportunities for exploratory jaunts on side roads, most of which offer at least one good view of the water—namely Blue Hill Bay. One such road is the Seal Cove Road, which runs from Southwest Harbor to Seal Cove. It takes you beside a series of turnoffs leading to the trailheads of Mansell, Bernard, and Western Mountains, from which you can look down on Long Pond and Seal Cove Pond as well as toward the sea. For a combination of woodland and seaside serenity, with picnic tables and an occasional gazebo thrown in, try the Pretty Marsh Picnic Area. It is open from 6:00 A.M. to 10:00 P.M. daily.

One of the most tranquil spots on the island is the Indian Point–Blagden Preserve off the Indian Point Road, which runs between Pretty Marsh and Town Hill. Operated by the Maine Chapter of The Nature Conservancy, the preserve has resident caretakers. The area in which the preserve is situated is one of the few areas on the island to have escaped the ravages of the 1947 fire. Islanders sometimes come here to escape the hubbub of the tourist season.

12
Schoodic Peninsula and Winter Harbor

One of the state's prime scenic areas is the Schoodic Peninsula, the portion of Acadia National Park located on the next large peninsula Down East from Mount Desert Island. The Schoodic Peninsula is just south of Winter Harbor, also home to a U.S. Navy intelligence base, which in conjunction with another base in Cutler monitors North Atlantic submarine traffic.

At the turn of the century and shortly afterward, the navy station and much of what would be the original summer population of Winter Harbor moved from Mount Desert Island to escape summer crowds. The navy, the summer people, and the tourists who now visit the Schoodic Peninsula annex of Acadia chose an enchanting place. The tiered garden of giant granite blocks that face the full run of the sea at Schoodic Point, the end of the peninsula, is a favorite local hangout during and after storms. Massive seas, one after another building from the horizon, surge forward to commit spectacular suicides against the rocks. During severe storms, spray from the crashing seas at Schoodic can fall in icy sheets over the forest several hundred yards back from the shore. But most days at Schoodic Point are as placid as the peninsula's beauty is striking, and the tigerish sea that can surge and seethe at its edge is as somnolent as a house cat.

Driving east from Schoodic Point on the loop road that circles the peninsula, beyond massive seawalls of cobbles hurled ashore by the ocean, are picnic sites facing Little Moose Island and, farther offshore, Schoodic Island. Sailboats often run between Schoodic Island and the mainland, which can be a visual treat. Little Moose is a serious island only at high tide. Wading over to it at low water is easy, but getting back when the tide has begun to flood can be risky. It is only about a twenty-yard swim across, but the combination of the swift current of a flooding tide and icy water is more than many people can handle.

The Acadia National Park section of the peninsula is still pretty much the way it was described in the 1950s by Louise Dickinson Rich in her best-selling book of the time, *The Peninsula*. One change from the 1950s is that the roadways, once surfaced with crushed pink granite, have been blacktopped. But, the residual pink granite is still visible along the road edges, wildflowers bloom unimpeded, and the views of Frenchman Bay are still splendid.

The Schoodic Peninsula, which is really the tip of a larger peninsula occupied by the Gouldsboros and Prospect Harbor, is on US 1 beyond the Hancock-Sullivan bridge, locally referred to as the "singing bridge" because of the sound of vehicle tires on its metal grate surface. The bridge was built in 1926 and carries US 1 over the Taunton River—not really a river at all but another tentacle of the sea that flows back and forth with the tide between Sullivan Harbor and Taunton Bay. You can glimpse part of the bay to the north as you cross the bridge. This whole end of Frenchman Bay, with its maze of islands and small estuaries, once offered hundreds of hiding places for eighteenth-century pirates as they lay in wait for prey.

East of Taunton Bay is 1,069-foot-high Schoodic Mountain, with sweeping views of Frenchman Bay and Mount Desert Island. To reach the trailhead from US 1, take State 200 (also known as the Bert Gray Road) to East Franklin. The best way to find the unmarked right turn to the trailhead in East Franklin is with an Appalachian Mountain Club Maine Mountain Guide, available at bookstores, or by asking directions on the way down the Bert Gray Road. Mainers are used to people asking directions.

Sullivan is named for Gen. Daniel Sullivan, who during the Revolution was the target of a small expeditionary force sent from the British garrison at Castine to capture him. He was captured, with help from local loyalists. Sullivan and other residents of upper Frenchman Bay had been building well-armed, shallow-draft vessels, which they used to attack British shipping. The vessel's hull configuration allowed them to be rowed at a fair speed in shoal water and be sailed moderately well in deep water. They were suited to Maine's large, island-studded estuaries. In any event, Crown forces, Loyalist merchant mariners, and fishermen did not like them much.

The town of Sullivan once had a nest of inns and lodges geared for the summer trade. It also had boardinghouses for the town's granite quarry workers and, later in the last century, for gold and silver miners who chose not to live in company boardinghouses. The quarrying and mining operations began shutting down at the end of the nineteenth century. The town's open spaces hint of its past industrial activity, which tends to give it a slightly tumbled down look.

Dunbar's Store, beside US 1 and next to one of the region's most scenic turnouts, occupies part of the space once taken up by the Waukeag Inn, which commanded a superb view of Frenchman Bay and Mount Desert Island. Dunbar's is a good spot to pick up a sandwich and a cup of coffee. Just beyond Dunbar's, on the right, is Sullivan's old stone store. The handsome granite building began life as a salt store in the last century. A short distance back from the store, on the edge of the bay, is the site of a former shipyard.

Sullivan's granite industry began in 1830. Sullivan granite was used to build the Hancock-Sullivan bridge, the stonework underpinnings of which are truly handsome.

The Sullivan end of the bridge is in line with a string of sites of former silver mines, which ran along the water from Sullivan Falls to North Sullivan. More silver mines, as well as copper mines, were strung along the northwestern shore of Taunton Bay above the bridge. Silver and gold mining ended in Sullivan in the 1880s with the discovery of the Comstock Lode near Virginia City, Nevada. The western silver veins were large, and mining in the West was easier and cheaper than it was in the East, particularly on the coast where saltwater intrusion into the mines was a hazard that made mining operations more expensive.

The cessation of mining in Sullivan coincided with the collapse of Maine's timber and shipbuilding industries. By the 1890s, the Waukeag Neck section of Sullivan became a summer playground. With some help from developers in Boston and Portsmouth, New Hampshire, Waukeag Neck residents successfully petitioned the legislature to become a separate community. It was named Sorrento by the developers, after the Italian city beside the Bay of Naples, and became a sister resort to Bar Harbor. Representatives of the upper echelons of the U.S. government once summered here. The Hotel Sorrento was a posh centerpiece of the resort where guests entertained themselves in billiard rooms and bowling alleys, and on tennis courts and croquet pitches that were ranked among the best in the nation. A freshwater supply was piped seven miles from the cluster of big hills called Schoodic Mountains, of which Schoodic Mountain is the highest; and a local electric company made Sorrento one of the most brightly lighted communities in North America, at least in summer.

Everyone arrived here by water. Passenger steamers plied Frenchman Bay between Bar Harbor, Hancock Point, Sullivan, Sorrento, and Winter Harbor. By 1896, Sorrento had become a popular yacht rendezvous, and yacht and canoe races were organized for Frenchman Bay. A legacy of the period is today's Frenchman Bay Regatta, an open race that is sponsored by the Bar Harbor and Sorrento Yacht Clubs. Ashore, Waukeag Neck's Gay Nineties summer residents were competing for the $1,000 Sorrento Tennis Cup.

There is nothing to suggest Sorrento's past when you turn south off US 1 onto State 185, the road to Sorrento. Just before the turnoff, if you are coming from the west, US 1 runs beside the head of Long Cove, where the state has set up some picnic tables. Keep an eye out for them and the sign for Sorrento. It is a tiny spot worthy of a look.

Sorrento has managed to decompress decorously from its glory days, and Mother Nature has framed some beautiful views of Frenchman Bay. Sorrento's harbor lies between Bean Point, which juts to the west of Waukeag Neck, and Dram and Preble Islands. Beyond is the wide expanse of often wind-whipped Frenchman Bay. On the west side of Bean Point is West Cove, where there is a boatyard of the same name. West Cove Boat Yard—a picturesque yard in a picturesque setting—maintains some finely fitted, classically designed sailing craft.

Much of Bean Point is taken up by what could be called downtown Sorrento, because that is where the post office is located amid a jumble of modest summer residences. The tree- and rock-strewn hillside that spills toward the harbor is overlaid by a broad latticework of roads laid out by the original developers. On the east side of Waukeag Neck is what is left of the Boss of the Bay gold mine, whose entrance faces Bass Cove and whose floor is flooded at high tide. On nearby Treasure Island, just offshore, is the site of the Golden Circle gold mine, whose shafts were filled long ago.

Another town that broke away from its parent is Winter Harbor, which separated from Gouldsboro in the 1890s and remains a summer retreat today, as well as the major town on the peninsula. Each August, Winter Harbor has a community festival, which has evolved in part as a consequence of the crowds drawn to the town by the lobster boat races. The festival lasts a weekend, the races just one day, unless fog alters their scheduling. The most popular vantage point for the races, other than on a boat in the harbor, is on the western side of the harbor at Frazier Point, where a lobster bake is provided at a price for race spectators. Race day can be one of the best times to visit the area. The atmosphere is that of a country fair, and the lobster dinners are good on palate and budget.

The eastern side of the harbor is formed by Grindstone Neck, where the type of stone used to make grindstones abounds, according to a local history. If local lore is to be believed, the neck's name derives from a shipwreck. The vessel that came to grief was carrying grindstones, which washed ashore along with the vessel's timbers.

Grindstone Neck is a beautiful place, its atmosphere chic although rustic. It is one of the region's last summer sanctuaries. The golf course and yacht club blend splendidly with the terrain; the houses along Grindstone Avenue look conspicuously elegant. At the end of Grindstone Avenue, shielded from the homes by evergreens, there is a turnaround with a strikingly pleasant view of harbor, bay, and sea. It is not a bad place to have a sandwich.

Winter Harbor entered the English-speaking world in the 1700s as Mosquito Harbor, a section of Gouldsboro. It has a supermarket, a full-service gas station, restaurants, general merchandise stores, a marina, and two boatbuilders.

Winter Harbor is on the loop of State 186, which at its western end meets US 1 in West Gouldsboro, and at its eastern end meets US 1 in Gouldsboro. The most prominently marked turnoff is in West Gouldsboro, with signs to the Schoodic portion of Acadia Natonal Park.

Along Main Street and State 186 in Winter Harbor is Chase's Restaurant, an old standby. The Donut Hole, at the edge of the head of the harbor, is a popular gathering spot, as is J. M. Gerrish, which dispenses sandwiches, ice cream, coffee, and soda pop with quiet charm near the intersection of Harbor Road and Main Street.

East of Winter Harbor on State 186 is Birch Harbor, at the head of a narrow inlet of the same name. According to local lore, it got its name from the stands of birch that once flourished there. Birch Harbor, one of three small communities in the town of Gouldsboro, is a favorite spot for watercolorists. Chipman's Store,

Prospect Harbor Light

at the head of the harbor, is a good spot to buy ready-made sandwiches. Across from Chipman's is a complex of buildings that includes the Country School House Restaurant.

Along the few miles from Birch Harbor to Prospect Harbor on State 186, a cluster of dilapidated dwellings with dooryard junk piles lets you know that the comparative opulence of Grindstone Neck is well astern. Tidy, modestly prosperous housing begins to appear as the road swings to the right and begins to descend seaward. As it snakes sharply left, a giant wooden outline of an oilskin-clad fisherman rises above the blue of the sea. This is Prospect Harbor, and rising above the fisherman's feet is the headquarters of Stinson Seafood Company, which packs and exports a variety of sardines and herring steaks.

Beyond is the harbor, where the fishing fleet is moored close enough to shore for a good look. Residences line either side of the road as far as Community Hall, which has been the site of many fishermen's meetings. Ray's Deli come into view at the center of the village, which is the juncture of State 186 and State 195. Prospect Harbor is a fishing village that still has much of its social fabric intact despite an influx of retirees and a few summer folk. The community and Stinson Seafood are linked economically. How Stinson fares depends on the annual herring run in the Gulf of Maine, as well as how the herring are running in the North Sea on the other side of the Atlantic. Poor herring catches on one side of the Atlantic can translate into marketing bonanzas on the opposite side. Adult herring are transformed into steaks and juvenile herring into sardines. When the runs of either or both have been poor in the North Sea, Stinson has boosted its shipments to Europe accordingly. When there is a poor run in the western Atlantic, Norway increases it shipments of sardines to North America. In the past, the company has welcomed visitors and provided tours when an employee had time to act as a guide.

The ocean has provided Prospect Harbor with its livelihood, and it has also provided it with a schoolhouse bell. In the late nineteenth century, a captain bound home to Gouldsboro came across a British registry vessel in distress, foundering on a reef off the Carolina coast. The vessel was the *Victoria* and she was laden with Cuban cigars that had been swayed aboard in Havana. The Mainers rescued the British crew, and the grateful Brits presented the Gouldsboro skipper with their ship's bell, which was an established custom of the sea. The Gouldsboro captain in turn presented the *Victoria's* bell to his town, and when a new schoolhouse was built the bell was hung in its belfry. Several generations of Gouldsboro schoolchildren grew up listening to the clang of the bell, until the old school was replaced by a new one and the bell was taken down. The Womens Club now has possession of the bell.

The *Victoria* may have gone down somewhat ignominiously while under charter to a British shipping firm, but she had a significant place in Canadian history. In 1864 when the United States was wrenching itself apart in a Civil War, what was to be Canada was being put together at a meeting of premiers at Charlottetown, Prince Edward Island. The premiers arrived aboard the *Victoria*, and at the conclusion of their meeting it was her bell that was rung to announce the agreement of confederation, which is somewhat equivalent to the United States' Declaration of Independence. When *Victoria's* bell tolled in Charlottetown Harbor, it became as much a symbol of Canadian nationalism as had the Liberty Bell at Philadelphia when it rang out to announce the signing of the Declaration of Independence.

The controversy over the *Victoria's* bell began in the 1980s when Canada was putting together a train to carry Canadian historical displays about the country. The Prospect Harbor Womens Club was approached about the return of the bell. They said no. The Canadian government sent an emissary to try to woo the bell away with charm and drink. The answer was still no. Canada briefly toyed with the idea of stealing the bell, but instead begged for its loan. The answer was the same and the effort fizzled. Canada decided to take a long-range approach and wait until the club's membership changed. The club in turn has put its bell away in a safe place. The incident of the bell was a big drama for a little town.

The most attractive feature in Prospect Harbor, other than the harbor itself, is its well-maintained lighthouse, at the end of Lighthouse Point Road. The lighthouse stands within a compound occupied by the Naval Satellite Operations Center, and the lighthouse is used as a retreat for navy personnel.

East of Prospect Harbor is Corea, a popular subject for painters and photographers, because it is one of the prettiest little fishing harbors on the coast. It is at the end of State 195. There is an attractive bed and breakfast—The Black Duck—on the way into town. The giant jungle gym–appearing apparatus rising above the scrub tree line on the right as you approach town is part of a navy communications system.

It's best to arrive in Corea with a full stomach, since there is only one commercial establishment, a tiny variety store, which is not always open; and finding a picnic spot requires ingenuity for anyone except the brazen.

Corea was settled in 1812 as Indian Harbor by Joseph Young, a seafarer and fisherman. The name Indian Harbor stuck until 1896, when the town got a post office and its name was changed.

Fishing boats, most kept in spiffy fashion, ride at their moorings in a somewhat circular harbor ringed by white clapboard homes. A church spire rises at the head of the harbor; at the foot of the harbor is a narrow slot running seaward between rock-faced, pine tree–covered Youngs Point and the mainland. Sunlight flashes through spray as seas crash on the offshore islands of Bar, Outer Bar, and Western. Beyond is the flat blue vastness of the Gulf of Maine. On the dirt road to Cranberry Point is Young Brothers, one of the state's prominent boatbuilders, whose buildings face the sea.

Corea, as it is now, is set for change. Poised above it is a large, half-built-on real estate development straggling along the west shore of Gouldsboro Bay with a small yacht club already in operation. It may be the seed of a population boom that the region's eighteenth-century promoters had sought unsuccessfully.

Development on this peninsula is not without precedent, as the town of Gouldsboro was founded by developers shortly after the American Revolution. The town got its start in 1764 when the land that was to be Gouldsboro was granted to three Bostonians: Nathan Jones, Francis Shaw, and Robert Gould. In 1790, Gould surveyed the land for the other principals with the idea of establishing a town. Gould's efforts at acquiring town status, such as including the names of dogs in census tallies, resulted in the town being named after him. During the same period a large section of Gouldsboro became part of the Bingham Estate, a vast timberland holding in eastern Maine that was managed from London. In 1795, Revolutionary War hero Gen. David Cobb, late of Gen. George Washington's staff, arrived in Gouldsboro as agent for the Bingham holdings. Cobb presided over the court at Castine when it was in session; when it was not, he busied himself with turning Gouldsboro into a city. It never happened, although Cobb apparently was better at attracting people to settle in Gouldsboro than Gould had been. The problem was that once people arrived in Gouldsboro they moved on to Ellsworth and Milbridge.

In 1820, John Black was sent out from London to take over management of the Bingham Estate from Genereal Cobb. Shortly afterward Black married one of Cobb's daughters, and the newly married couple, just as so many others had done, moved to Ellsworth, where they built what came to be called the Black Mansion.

13
Steuben
to Jonesport

If you have time and believe that bleak can be beautiful, then Washington County will be your oyster. You can consume hours threading your way down the back roads leading to hundreds of necks and peninsulas that run every which way into a watery jumble of small estuaries. The coastal scenery is among the most beautiful in the state. It is a low-lying coastline with marshes, meandering streams and rivers, and cobble and sand beaches. It has a much softer feel than the starkly dramatic landscapes of Mount Desert Island. Certainly the people, despite the region's harsh economy, can be among the nicest to be encountered between Kittery and Calais.

The region's blueberry barrens can be bleak (it is a matter of individual taste), but the true bleakness of Washington County is its poverty. Unemployment can run as high as 20 percent and last for far longer than it takes rain and sun to turn the seasonally burned-over blueberry barrens green, or for the annual return of the herring. The clapboards of pristine, Federal houses in Washington County have been weathered free of paint, and the only sign of habitation is often freshly washed clothing hung on a line, billowing in the wind.

Rather than reflecting the way life should be, to borrow Maine's slogan, Washington County reflects the way life became after the collapse of the shipbuilding and timber industries in the state, and the way life would have continued to be for much of the rest of Maine if alternative industries had not been developed.

Washington County has enterprise, but it is at the eastern end of Maine, with a natural economic and cultural affinity with Canada but separated from it by the international border. And its ports are the farthest in Maine from the abundant fishing grounds of Georges Bank. The Gulf of Maine is somewhat wedge-shaped with Georges Bank as the base and one side of the acute-angled tip washing against the Washington County shoreline. The other side of the tip was bent sharply inward in the early 1980s when the International Court of Justice at The Hague, The Netherlands, drew a new international boundary line for the Gulf of Maine, awarding Canada a choice part of Georges Bank, known as the Northeast Peak. Rich in scallops, lobsters, and groundfish, and just over the horizon from Washington County ports, the popularly called Hague Line now denies the region's fishermen access to Canadian waters that they had once fished through gentlemen's agreements with their counterparts to the east. That is not an explanation of why Washington County is poor, just that it lacks political clout because it is poor, and because it lacks clout the county is often forgotten in Augusta and Washington when state and federal dollars are passed around.

Regardless of all that, there are attractive communities in Washington County, the village of Steuben being one of them.

Named for Baron von Steuben, the German mercenary who at Valley Forge, Pennsylvania, during the Revolution drafted what was to become the basis for the U.S. Army's Manual of Arms, the village is partially visible across a clearing from US 1. Road signs at either end of Steuben indicate where to turn off for what can amount to a ten- to fifteen-minute loop through a scattered nest of some of the most charming eighteenth- and nineteenth-century houses along the coast. East of the village on US 1 are two fingers of land that point seaward—Dyer Neck and Petit Manan Point.

Dyer Neck forms the east shore of Gouldsboro Bay and the west shore of Dyer Bay, which runs north toward Steuben village.

It is worth a drive down Dyer Neck's Morgador Road to get as close as you can to Dyer Point, but the richest reward for your efforts is a tour of Petit Manan Point, which forms the eastern shore of Dyer Bay. It is reached from the Pigeon Hill Road off US 1.

The nearly 2,000 acres of Petit Manan Point make up roughly two-thirds of the Petit Manan National Wildlife Refuge, which includes Petit Manan Island (where Petit Manan Light is located) and Bois Bubert and Nash Islands. Part of the mainland, Petit Manan Point has footpaths that lead through spruce forests and along ten miles of windswept shoreline, cedar swamps, cobble beaches, saltwater marshes, and heaths. The refuge is maintained by the U.S. Department of the Interior's Fish and Wildlife Service to assure way stations for migrating birds. Petit Manan Island, with a 100-foot-high light tower, is a haven for ospreys, eagles, puffins, razorbills, guillemots, and a variety of gulls. Hiking on the shore anywhere in the refuge during nesting season is taboo.

Having a kayak or canoe lashed to your vehicle's roof will get you to relatively close Bois Bubert Island. But more distant Nash and Petit Manan Islands lie in different directions several miles offshore in open sea. The sea between Petit Manan Point and Petit Manan Island is almost always dangerous. An underwater ledge runs between the two, and off Petit Manan Island high rock pinnacles rise toward the surface from the sea floor. The result is an almost constantly confused sea that can cause boats steered by experienced seamen to suddenly alter course. All of which are good reasons to call or drop by the refuge office in Milbridge, about half an hour's drive from Steuben.

Milbridge, a former shipbuilding center on the Narraguagus River, is popular with sportfishermen in pursuit of Atlantic salmon, so popular at times that local sportfishermen complain of shoulder-to-shoulder fishermen lining the banks.

Milbridge is now a sardine and blueberry processing center and a local entertainment and shopping center. The supermarket makes excellent sandwiches to order. There is a movie theater

Superbly adapted for swimming,
puffins seem to walk on land with a sailor's roll

and a seasonal legitimate theater. The Red Barn restaurant and motel, located in the center of town, is something of an unofficial Down East meeting center for businesspeople. It has excellent pies, puddings, and chowders. Milbridge and environs is becoming increasingly popular, and along Main Street there are now a number of bed and breakfasts.

On the way into town, Wyman Road off US 1 leads down the western shore of Narraguagus Bay to McLellan Park. The Wyman Road is about a hundred yards beyond a "shipshape and Bristol fashion" Victorian mansion with large windows that marks the entrance to Milbridge. Directly ahead at the intersection is the utilitarian outline of the sardine factory, partially hidden behind a white church. McLellan Park looks out over a softly beautiful bay that can be suffused with pastel colors.

At the opposite end of Milbridge, US 1 makes a ninety-degree turn just before the Red Barn and is carried over the Narraguagus River on a pontoon-style bridge whose western end can pivot on a piling to allow boat traffic to pass up and down the river. It was last opened in the 1980s to allow a passenger schooner built in a field upriver to pass to the sea. The launching was something of an unplanned reenactment of what was once a common occurrence along the Narraguagus, and a lot of cheering was in tribute to a recollected past.

Across the river from Milbridge, just over the bridge and visible from it, is a road leading to a public boat launching ramp used by fishermen and pleasure boaters. Farther along US 1 and running off to the left, paralleling the Narraguagus, is the Kansas Road, which straggles through back country on its several-mile wind to Cherryfield, a pleasing blueberry- and pulpwood-processing center.

East of Cherryfield and Milbridge, just off US 1 on the Harrington River, is the town of Harrington. As is Cherryfield, Harrington has the look of a nice, quiet place to live, but for a visitor there is not a lot to do. Harrington does have a wreath-making factory, which is open for tours, and around Harrington there are nearly fifty trout-fishing streams.

Farther east, where the Pleasant River flows under a bridge supporting US 1, is the village of Columbia Falls, whose major advertised attraction is Ruggles House and its finely hand-carved interior. Built in 1818, the interior of the Federal-style house sports a flying staircase. Intricately carved woodwork replete with delicately rendered garlands and flowers adorns the rooms. Ruggles House is open seasonally and there is an admission fee.

The village of Addison lies below Columbia Falls on the Pleasant River, which forms a series of oxbows as it meanders between the two towns before spilling out into a broad stream just below Addison village. The bays and small estuaries between Milbridge and Addison make up a sea kayakers' and canoeists' playground. The town of Addison slopes gently toward the sea. The road from Addison village to South Addison village trends along the east bank of the Pleasant River.

At South Addison the road bends onto Moose Neck and unravels like a rope into a series of dead ends, some of which provide views of Nash Island Light, offshore. The region is another favorite of painters and photographers, and nearby Cape Split is dotted with artists' summer residences.

With Moose Neck, Cape Split forms Cape Split Harbor, one of the best harbors between Northeast Harbor, on Mount Desert Island, and the Canadian border. It is also one of the most softly beautiful places on the coast. Cape Split in particular is beautiful, but it has been developed by a land company and the result is that driving around Cape Split can make you more concerned about violating the privacy of the residents than in viewing leaf-filtered seascapes.

The next town Down East from Addison is Jonesport, which sprouts along the northern shore of Moosabec Reach. This lobster-fishing and sardine-canning town has one of the best small-town Fourth of July parades on the coast in which the whole town participates as either marchers or spectators. Main Street residents gather on their front lawns to watch the paraders, many of them lifelong friends and relatives, pass by on foot and on floats. Later, paraders and spectators join the serious attraction of the day, which is the annual Jonesport-Beals Lobster Boat Races in Moosabec Reach. The town of Beals, made up of Beals Island and Great Wass Island, forms the southern limit of Moosabec Reach, a stretch of saltwater that is a shared thoroughfare of both communities, which are connected by a green bridge that arcs skyward.

Spectators, two and three deep on the bridge footpath, crowd against the rail to watch the mile-long race. It is the town's biggest event of the year, and some of the fishing boats running the course are the handsomest in the state. Jonesport and Beals are traditional fishing communities, and well-designed boats and good boatbuilders enjoy the same appreciation that good horses and good horse breeders enjoy in Kentucky.

Jonesport is the home of the Jonesporter lobster boat, a design that began to evolve on both sides of the reach in the 1930s and 1940s and continues to be modified and refined by skilled local designers. The Jonesporter, with its high bow and square stern, has become something of a standard for Down East lobster boats. When you see a photograph of a lobster boat on a restaurant placemat, it is more often than not a Jonesporter or a Jonesporter-inspired design.

14
Way Down East:
Machias
to Eastport

The waters of the Gulf of Maine and the Bay of Fundy commingle in this region, where the mighty St. Croix River floods seaward between the United States and Canada. Off Eastport is Old Sow, the largest whirlpool in the Western Hemisphere, its ferocity second in the world only to that of Norway's Maelstrom. This is border country, where United States and Canadian cultures merge with the fluidity of the St. Croix and the offshore waters, forming a little country of its own, bounded roughly on the west by Machias—Washington County's shiretown—and to the east by Calais, Lubec, Eastport, and Campobello Island. The region is a paradise for naturalists, who explore its intricate bays and estuaries in kayaks and canoes and tread its shorelines on foot. In winter, nature trails are open to cross-country skiers and snowshoers.

The region is the least visited on the coast and, maybe because of that, the most pleasant to tour. Machias is a good beginning point, certainly the most logical if you are coming from the west.

The shiretown and the Machias River, which flows through it, were once almost as famous for spring timber drives as Bangor's Penobscot. The Machias River's hinterland is still one of the most active logging regions in the state. The Chamber of Commerce does not boast about it, but Machias was first settled as a seventeenth-century pirate outpost before becoming a respectable trading community. The town's first successful settlement dates from 1763, most of the fly-by-night pirates who attempted their own form of settlement in the previous century having been hanged in Boston.

The rural city's origins as a criminal fortress are lightly skimmed over in favor of it being the site of the first naval engagement of the American Revolution. The watery skirmish occurred in 1776, two months after the Battle of Lexington (Massachusetts), and the details of both blood-tinged incidents are suspended in a scholarly tug-of-war between the school of disinterested historical accuracy and the school of partisan American patriotism. The United States version of the fight is that the British Royal Navy vessel *Margaretta,* which had been one of several war vessels convoying two Loyalist Machias merchant vessels back to their homeport from Boston, was captured in a daring action by fiercely patriotic local residents led by Capt. Jeremiah O'Brien. The very different Loyalist version is that O'Brien was a ringleader of drunken, dockside rowdies who set upon a British midshipman in charge of a tender that had been sent ashore to gather provisions. It remains for historical purists to ferret out the true story. In any event the master of the *Margaretta* died from his wounds in Machias's Burnham Tavern, where he was brought following the sea fight. The tavern is the oldest building east of Bangor and is now a museum maintained by the Daughters of the American Revolution.

The westerly approach to Machias on US 1 is through an expanse of blueberry barrens, which are burned off in early spring, turn sharply green in summer, and fade to russet in winter. Take a few scenically rewarding meanders before arriving in town.

Coming from Jonesport you can follow State 187 along the shoreline of Englishman Bay (named for English men-o-war that once lurked there). Sandy River Beach, a few miles outside of Jonesport, faces Roque Island and Roque Bluffs State Park (more about that later). State 187 merges with US 1 west of Jonesboro, beside the Chandler River, which flows into Englishman Bay.

Jonesboro, on US 1 a few miles outside of Machias, is named for John Coffin Jones, who received 48,160 acres from the American government as compensation for the loss of his sloop in 1779, during the siege of the British garrison at Castine. Jones's tract included Roque Bluffs, noted for its beauty, and extended from Bucks Harbor below Machias to the present town of Jonesboro. In Jonesboro are the ruins of a mill dam that once harnessed the power of the Chandler River.

Either keep going to Machias, if you are in a hurry, or do a much more preferable thing: take the first right after crossing the Chandler River and head down to 300-acre Roque Bluffs State Park. If you took State 187 from Jonesport, you already squinted at Roque Bluffs from Sandy River Beach on the west side of Englishman Bay. Roque Island is a favorite anchorage of the New York Yacht Club during its summer cruise to Maine. The park contains that rarity of rarities in Maine—sand dunes, albeit small ones—and a sandy beach that faces Roque Island. A freshwater pond provides an option to swimming in saltwater. The park is one of the prettiest public places in the state and well worth taking the time to enjoy before continuing to Machias, which, if you have a road map, you can do over back roads. Whichever way you choose to go—either back to Jonesboro on the Roque Bluffs Road or up to the immediate outskirts of Machias on the other section of the Roque Bluffs Road—you will come out on US 1.

Machias may be close to saltwater, but it is more of a jumping-off spot for freshwater sportfishermen, swimmers, and boaters, many of whom come into the city through the Machias Valley Airport and then head inland to a network of lakes, ponds, and streams. The airport is on the westerly approach to Machias. Just beyond, perched on a hill overlooking the Machias River and downtown Machias, is a University of Maine campus, which was originally established as a teachers' college in 1909. The university offers courses in marine biology (among other things) and uses the county's extensive coastline as an outdoor

Lobster traps with their buoys

laboratory. The state's university system also maintains Blueberry Hill Experimental Farm beside US 1 in Jonesboro.

Machias is worth poking about. The downtown is clean and orderly, and shows signs of economic rejuvenation with such enterprises as the large, clapboard, thirty-shop complex called Ferris Wheel Emporium and such small nearby shops as the Sow's Ear, which comes into view as you cross the Machias River bridge. At an acute diagonal across from the Ferris Wheel

Emporium is the mustard-colored Burnham Tavern with its gambrel roof. Radiating away from downtown along tree-lined residential streets like so many marching columns are white painted houses, many with lush flower and vegetable gardens. Machias has a homey feel to it but also an inland flavor.

If you are looking for a sense of serenity with a salty tang, turn right on State 92 and head down toward Machiasport, whose borders include Bucks Harbor and Starboard, two of the most picturesque and least populated communities on the coast.

On the left not much more than a hundred yards after turning into State 92 are Bad Little Falls Park and Overlook, the South Shore Path, and the O'Brien Cemetery. You can look down at the wildly cascading falls of the Machias River from a wooden footbridge and then follow beside the roiling torrent on the South Shore Path to O'Brien Cemetery.

Back on the road, immediately past the falls, is a charming residential district of period houses. Then there is not a lot to see until you get to Fort O'Brien State Park, which overlooks the confluence of the Machias River and Machias Bay. The ride through Bucks Harbor along Machias Bay and down to Starboard, where the bay meets the Gulf of Maine, is one of the most scenically attractive in the state. The little lobster-fishing port of Cutler can be glimpsed far across the bay to the east. Cutler, for all its simplicity, is the site of one of the world's most powerful communications systems. Those nearly thousand-foot high towers that rise like colossal red range poles are used by the U.S. Navy to communicate with the U.S. Fleet in the North Atlantic, Europe, and the Arctic. The towers lend a futuristic touch to the sweeping land and seascapes on the drive to Starboard. The 2,800-acre navy base at Cutler (except for the towers, you can see nothing but trees and water) was established in 1960 when the cold war was hot and Allied and Soviet submarines engaged in tense confrontations in the North Atlantic.

Starboard is picture perfect, but it too is not without blemish. Just outside the village, and out of sight till you round a curve in the road and begin heading downhill to Jasper Beach, is a maximum-security prison set on a rocky crag like a fortress. Discovering it is like coming across a skunk in a garden. It is part of life, but the unexpected encounter is a jolt.

Offshore, if you can pick it out, is Libby Island Light, marking the approach to Machias Bay. Jasper Beach, at the end of a short, rutted road, is worth a look. The beach is named for the mounded seawall of smooth blackish green jasper stones that stretch along the shore. The way back to Machias is on the same road you came.

East Machias, which is strung out along the East Machias River, has some interesting architecture despite a nineteenth-century exodus. In the late 1800s, when it was clear that Maine's timber industry was collapsing, residents of East Machias went to Washington state where beside the Hood Canal near Puget Sound they recreated their former town and called it Port Gamble.

From East Machias eastward, because of the broad indentation made by Cobscook Bay, US 1 begins to bend inland. So in East Machias turn off US 1 onto State 191, otherwise called the Cutler Road. It follows the shore up to West Lubec, passing some superb vistas of Grand Manan Channel.

By the time you get to Lubec you will feel you have arrived in a near hive of activity. The best way to enhance and maintain that feeling about Lubec is to cross the Roosevelt International Bridge to Campobello Island, New Brunswick, and look back from the hillside parking lot of the Canadian Tourist Information Centre. With a favorable vantage point and the benefit of detail-blurring distance, Lubec and its sister city, Eastport, the two most easterly communities in the United States, seem like picture-book villages.

Lubec is the easternmost city in the United States (it beats out Eastport by three-quarters of a mile). Lubec and Eastport face each other from opposite sides of the three-mile-wide entrance to Cobscook Bay. The bay balloons inland, its hundreds of necks and islands creating a great watery maze that can be a heaven for experienced sea kayakers, canoeists, and small boat sailors. It can be dangerous for the inexperienced because of the strong tides that surge through the bay's smaller inlets, turning them into boiling rapids.

Lubec is a fishing community where there were once twenty sardine-packing plants. Now there are two, and downtown Lubec, for all its pristine architectural charm, has a look of economic hard times. Yet there is a growing number of bed and breakfasts in a small patchwork of narrow, residential streets. You can walk around the most interesting parts of downtown in about an hour or less.

The Sardine Village Museum, on the way out of town, is a good place to see the history of this industry. Also on the way out of town is the reason many people come to Lubec, 481-acre West Quoddy Head State Park, at the end of the South Lubec Road. Here the red-and-white–striped West Quoddy Head Light, built in 1808, faces the southwestern tip of Campobello Island across Lubec Channel. The light stands on the easternmost point of the United States mainland. In the distance are the sharply chiseled cliffs of Canada's Grand Manan Island, a commercial fishing island that is a popular gathering spot for bird-watchers from around the world.

The park has a picnic ground and a hiking trail that winds along the shore. Next to the park is Carrying Place Cove, a National Natural Landmark, which is considered the finest example of a coastal raised-plateau bog in the United States. On the road to the lighthouse is West Quoddy Biological Research Station, a nonprofit organization offering Bay of Fundy nature studies and operating a rescue clinic for marine mammals and birds.

Whales (right, finback, humpback, and minke) are a common sight in the region, and whale-watching, island-hopping, and bird-watching boat trips are available in Lubec. You can also whale watch ashore at West Quoddy Head and East Quoddy Head on Campobello from early spring through late fall. One of the most popular charter boat trips is to the puffin nesting ground on Machias Seal Island. Other members of the region's bird population include razorbills, northern phalaropes, Arctic terns, Bonaparte gulls, great blue herons, bald eagles, and osprey. For those who like to go near the water but not on it, the break-water on the Johnson Bay side of Lubec, facing the entrance to Cobscook Bay, is a favorite spot to watch the tide race by at a speed of six to eight knots. Lubec is at the lower end of the Bay of Fundy, where tides can rise and fall as much as thirty feet and fog is commonplace.

Another reason many people come to Lubec is to get to Campobello Island, the site of former President Franklin D. Roosevelt's summer residence. Despite the international border, Lubec, Campobello Island, and Eastport form three sections of what in many ways is one community. The people share a common heritage, work together, play together, and marry one another.

Campobello is not as big nor as naturally dramatic as Mount Desert Island, but the views from it are among the most lovely on the coast. The big attraction is 500-acre Roosevelt Campobello International Park, which includes Roosevelt's former home. The rambling, rustic, deep-red cottage near the fishing village of Welshpool faces Eastport across the swirling blue plain of Friar Roads. Popular vantage points in the park are Liberty Head and the picnic grounds at Grassy Point, Raccoon Beach, and Herring Cove Beach.

One of the best seascapes on the island is at East Quoddy Head Lighthouse, which stands on a granite skerry overlooking the open sea to the east, Eastport to the west, and, to the north, Deer Island amid the distant stretch of Passamaquoddy Bay. Whales are a common sight off East Quoddy Head. A considerate person has placed a pickup truck seat on the promontory for ease of seascape viewing. It is much more comfortable than a government bench.

In addition to its small fishing villages, Campobello has a small summer colony and a golf course. A surprise of sorts inland of Welshpool are the partially completed roads and cleared lots of a collapsed real estate development that figured peripherally in the investigation of the so-called Whitewater Scandal involving Arkansas real estate wheelers and dealers when President Clinton was governor of Arkansas. The failed development on Campobello probably has more to do with the inability of salesmen to induce Arkansans to buy summer homes on Campobello than it does with understanding the scope of Whitewater. Most of the house lots appear to have poor drainage.

In July and August a ferry runs from Campobello, past Eastport, to Deer Island, New Brunswick, which is considered a very pleasant place to visit, and the ferry ride provides a chance to look at the swirling waters of Old Sow.

Eastport is only three miles from Lubec by water and two miles from Campobello, but to get to it by motor vehicle requires driving forty miles around Cobscook Bay. To get there, reverse direction on State 189 from Lubec and at Whiting turn right into US 1. Just beyond Whiting on Whiting Bay, which is part of the maze of Cobscook Bay, is Cobscook Bay State Park. It is set up for camping, picnicking, fishing, swimming, boating, and, in winter, cross-country skiing and snowmobiling. Just beyond is the Edmunds Unit of Moosehorn National Wildlife Refuge. The Edmunds Unit, and the much larger Baring Unit of the refuge, outside of Calais, have miles of roads that are closed to motor vehicles but are open for hiking, cross-country skiing, and snowmobiling. Refuge headquarters is just outside of Calais. Find a telephone book and call the refuge manager about the rules for visiting the Edmunds Unit.

The US 1 loop around Cobscook Bay leads through Dennysville and Pembroke—both rich in logging history—and finally Perry (named for Commodore Oliver H. Perry, who defeated a British fleet on Lake Erie in the War of 1812). At Perry, State 190 leaves US 1 and runs down a long finger of land to Eastport. Just before Eastport is the Pleasant Point State Indian Reservation, where much of the Passamaquoddy Nation resides and whose presence explains the scattering of Indian-ware shops in Perry and along State 190.

Eastport, which is on Moose Island, was settled by fishermen in 1782, became a major smuggling port during the War of 1812, and in the 1870s began the state's sardine industry when the price of the then-popular, oil-fried French sardines skyrocketed in the United States, as a consequence of the Franco-Prussian War. Maine's first sardine cannery opened in Eastport in 1873 to fill the market gap created by runaway French sardine prices. The city remains an inshore and offshore fishing port; it has also become the center of a growing aquaculture industry, which pen-rears salmon and sea trout for restaurants on the East Coast. Because of its deepwater harbor, Eastport has become a topping-off port for 800-foot-long, trans-Atlantic ships hauling forest products and paper-making materials between the Americas, the British Isles, and continental Europe.

Economic recovery, partly because of renewed shipping activity, began to seep slowly into Eastport in the 1980s, but it came too late to save most of its handsome, massively timbered, downtown commercial buildings that once backed up to the sea and gracefully faced Main Street. Victims of neglect, they fell down or burned down. With their loss went most of the downtown's visual reminders of its nineteenth-century maritime prosperity and most of the downtown's aesthetic charm, although Eastport is an interesting and attractive small city. Inns and bed and breakfasts have been emerging here like mushrooms. With huge amounts of restoration money it could excel Marblehead or Edgartown, Massachusetts, in architectural integrity and grace.

The city's maritime past and present are reflected in the state-funded Maine Marine Trades Center, beside Cobscook

Bay, which offers excellent courses in boatbuilding materials and techniques, boat repair, and boat design. The center is a satellite of Washington County Technical College in Calais, and its graduates are prized by Maine boatbuilders, who rank the center as the best boatbuilding school in the state. The school is open to visitors.

Eastport's location shaped its early history. Before and during the War of 1812, Eastport, along with the rest of eastern Maine, was a major smuggling arena from which much of the remainder of the East Coast benefited. When President Thomas Jefferson placed an embargo on American shipping in 1807 in an attempt to avoid war with England or France, it was Eastport, which lay cheek by jowl with what then remained of British North America, that was the salvation of financially desperate shippers. Hundreds of thousands of barrels of flour and other produce were hauled to Eastport. Every conceivable boat lined the beaches at night to ferry the contraband the short distance to Campobello and Grand Manan Island and to waiting British ships in Passamaquoddy Bay. Profits for a short two-mile row to Campobello were as high as 300 percent.

The most interesting stretch of US 1 in the state is between Perry and Calais. There are sweeping views of Passamaquoddy Bay with repeated glimpses of St. Andrews, New Brunswick—the Crown-established fishing village to which the United Empire Loyalists from Castine and other Loyalist centers fled in 1783 when the Revolution ended. Many had their houses dismantled by the British army, which reassembled them along the newly laid out streets of St. Andrews. Several of the original houses that were brought from Castine are still standing, as well as Robert Pagan's store, which once stood in downtown Castine. During Castine's bicentennial reenactment of the Penobscot Expedition in 1979, St. Andrews residents journeyed to Castine by automobile and boat to take part in the commemoration. Castine residents planted marigolds, a Loyalist symbol, around their houses as a salute to those who had fled 200 years before. St. Andrews is well worth a visit if you have the time.

At Robbinston, about halfway between Perry and Calais on US 1, you begin running beside the St. Croix River rather than Passamaquoddy Bay. Redclyffe Shore Motel and Dining Room appears on the right overlooking the river. The dining room and office are housed in a wooden gingerbread Victorian house whose sharply sloping roof is accentuated by large bargeboards. The effect is somewhat Old World, and the dining room gives views of the river and bay. Each room has an ocean view and there is a veranda beside the water.

At Red Beach, about halfway between Robbinston and Calais, the evergreen-tufted St. Croix Island, the site of the first Christmas celebration in North America, rises from the river. Now a state park, the 1604–05 French settlement, established on the island by Samuel de Champlain and Sieur de Monts, has been restored. Using the island as a base, the two explorers charted the coast as far south as Cape Cod.

The first signs of Calais are a golf course by the river, followed by large well-kept houses and then a more compact residential section of Victorian gingerbread houses. The first settlers came here from Ireland, Massachusetts, and Jonesport.

During the second quarter of the nineteenth century, Calais (pronounced CAL us) was a boomtown with thirty-six sawmills in operation and 272 vessels engaged in the lumber trade. With vast quantities of lumber and a demand for ships, Calais was also a shipbuilding town, which supplied small, two-masted lumber schooners for clients on either side of the St. Croix. The schooners were designed to bottom out stably on the mudflats when the ebb tide in the St. Croix dropped its water level twenty-three feet.

Despite a fire in 1870 that destroyed most of downtown along with its piers, Calais achieved its zenith of prosperity in

1874, when there were 1,169 vessel arrivals and 1,177 vessel departures. Today the city is a manufacturing, transportation, and recreation hub.

With 4,000 residents, Calais is the largest city in Washington County, and with its sister city of St. Stephen, New Brunswick, directly across the St. Croix, it has the region's largest population. The two cities are connected by a bridge. Calais is the fifth busiest port of entry to the United States on the Canadian border, nearly 2 million vehicles entering the United States through Calais annually. Each year the residents of Calais and St. Stephen join in an International Festival, from the first Saturday through the second Sunday in August.

Calais has the most amenities in the region: good restaurants, pleasant places to stay, a sprinkling of interesting retail shops and buildings, boat charters, and a well-run State of Maine Tourist Information Center, at the foot of North Street, where there is a walkway beside the river.

Southwest of Calais, off State 9, is the Moosehorn National Wildlife Refuge Baring Unit and headquarters. This breeding ground for migratory birds and other wildlife was established in 1937 as the first in a chain of such refuges extending from Maine to Florida. (If you found a public telephone in Edmunds, you know all about it.) The refuge in the 1800s was alive with logging activity. Timber was piled along the banks of the St. Croix in winter to be floated down to Calais in the spring. Now new forest conceals traces of former industry, as well as farms that once existed to feed the loggers. Refuge hikers still find cellar holes and stone fences in the woods.

Index